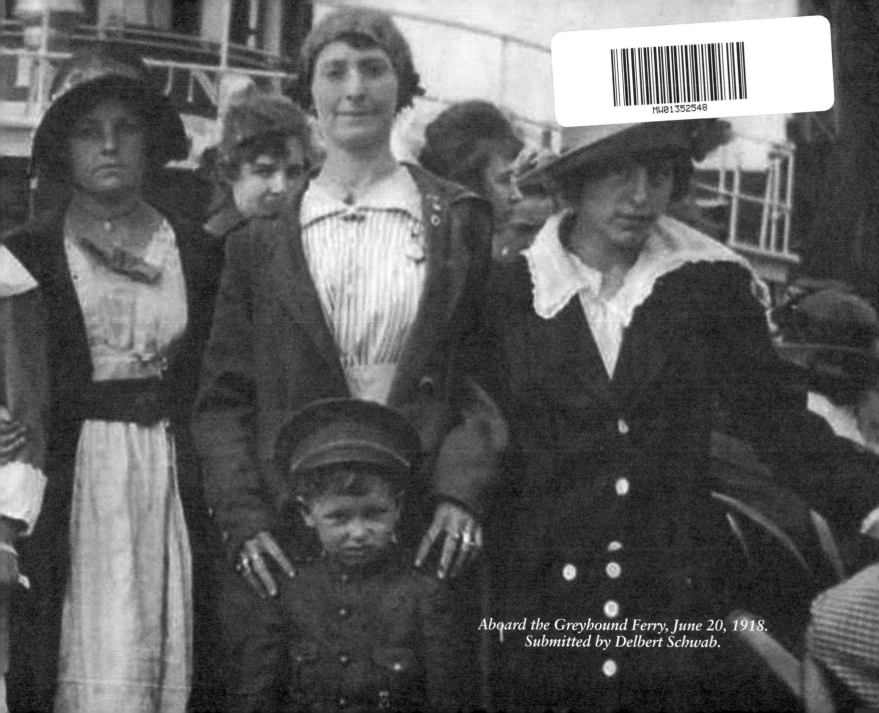

*Aboard the Greyhound Ferry, June 20, 1918.
Submitted by Delbert Schwab.*

TOLEDO

Our Life, Our Times, Our Town, Vol. II

1800s – 1960 Toledo, Ohio

John Robinson Block
Publisher & Editor in Chief, The Blade

Joseph H. Zerbey, IV
Vice President & General Manager

Kelly J. Norwood
Project Manager

Sara E. Welborn
Creative Director/Graphic Designer

THE BLADE
toledoblade.com®

COVER PHOTOGRAPH.
Lucas County Courthouse circa early 1900s.

Lucas County was created by the Ohio legislature in 1835 with Toledo as the county seat. However, at the time, Maumee was growing faster than Toledo and the county government moved there in 1840. A courthouse was built on River Road on the site of Dudley's Massacre where the Maumee library is now located. But by 1852, as Toledo's population increased dramatically, the county seat was moved back downtown and a three-story brick courthouse was built on the corner of Erie and Adams Streets. On September 3, 1893, Lucas County laid the cornerstone for a new courthouse on Adams behind the old 1852 building. The beautiful new courthouse of classical Roman architecture was designed by David L. Stine, the Toledo architect who also designed Scott and Waite high schools, and was built at a cost of $500,000. Because the Courthouse Square was originally swampy ground in Toledo's early "Frog Town" days, a mosaic of a frog was inlaid in the terrazzo floor at the Adams Street entrance. On January 1, 1897, about 40,000 visitors toured the courthouse at its formal dedication.

Submitted by Sharon Yaros

The Blade 2006

Many monuments have been added over the years to the courthouse and the courthouse mall. Dedicated in 1903, Ohio's first monument honoring Ohio-born President William McKinley stands near the entrance on Adams Street. And in 1925 on the Jackson Street side, a statue of "citizen soldier" was dedicated honoring all from Toledo and Lucas County who fought in the Spanish American war.

To celebrate its 100th anniversary, the building received a modern cleaning and upgrade, and remains one of the architectural gems of the county.

Copyright © 2006 by The Blade
ISBN 0-9770681-1-0

Published by The Blade
A Block Communications Company
541 North Superior Street
Toledo OH 43660
Printed in the United States of America

For General Information, Customer Service, and Orders Contact:
Telephone   419.724.6545
                    800.245.3317
FAX   419.724.6080
E-Mail   historybook@toledoblade.com

FOREWORD

When we first asked area residents to search through their treasured photos of times past, we had no idea their pictures would become everyone's treasures! But they have. Last year's publication of **Toledo, Our Life, Our Times, Our Town** was warmly received and quickly sold out.

Today, I am proud to introduce Volume II of this exciting pictorial series. As in our previous book, it reveals a way of life long gone – but that beats on in the hearts of all who lived through those years or heard about them from parents and grandparents.

Literally hundreds of current and former residents of Toledo rummaged through their attics, trunks and albums to provide this photographic history of their home town. Under the masterful hand of project manager Kelly J. Norwood and creative director Sara E. Welborn, their submissions were evaluated and assembled into the second edition of a series we hope becomes a much-loved memento for many generations to come. We've even added another decade to the timeline – the booming 1950s – to enhance the book's depth and interest.

This is more than a photo album of a city; it is a portrait of Toledo at work and at play, at war and in peace, dressed up to celebrate its finest hours and dressed down to tackle its toughest times. You'll see people, places and proceedings you forgot existed – or thought only existed in the stories told at a relative's knee. Downtown businesses, uptown socialites and everything in between – rich with details that tug at the heartstrings. Dirt streets, picket fences, dainty prams, dapper derbies, satin hair bows and shining smiles: snapshots you have never seen before and never will again.

If you own Volume I of **Toledo, Our Life, Our Times, Our Town**, you'll be thrilled to add Volume II to your collection. If you do not, now is the time to start a tradition. Purchase one of these exciting mementoes for everyone in your family, and share the laughter and tears of remembering.

Rest assured, this series is already a treasured tradition for all of us here at The Blade!

Joseph H. Zerbey, IV
Vice President & General Manager
The Blade

ACKNOWLEDGEMENT

We wish to acknowledge the generosity of our readers who have graciously once again entrusted us with their photographs of people at home, at work, and at play and scenes of Toledo and its surrounding communities. We have assembled these into a second volume that is unique in format and features photographs, most of which have not previously been published.

We have presented each photograph with a short caption that tells its story. In most cases, we have relied upon the information shared with us by the donor for this purpose. For some, we have provided supplemental research and have included a bibliography of the sources consulted. An index of all the historical surnames mentioned in the captions is included along with a listing of all those who contributed photographs to this volume. The photographs are old, sometimes have not been well cared for, or have even been abused. For the most part, we present them as they came to us, with tears, folds and other damage. We consider these imperfections to be a part of the pictures themselves.

Writing and Research
Larry R. Michaels
Doreen Robideaux

Writing
Denise Meyer
John R. Husman
Kelly J. Norwood
Lisa Lawrence
Jane Bryan Welborn
Sara E. Welborn
Annie Cieslukowski
Fred Folger

Contributing Graphic Designer
Phillip D. Long

Coordinator
Matthew T. Lentz

Additional Thanks
Jim Marshall, *Retired Manager of The Toledo-Lucas County Public Library, Local History and Genealogy Department and the great library staff*
Pam Griesinger, Blade IT, *for her computer expertise*
Neilah Kirchner, *for her trusted proofreading ability*
The Blade Library, Toledo Lucas County Port Authority,
Toledo's Attic, Tedd Long, The Toledo Firefighter's Museum

MUST BE A BIG SALE.

Main Street in East Toledo was still called Bridge Street when this photo of the Plumey Block was taken about 1880. Built in 1874, and named for early merchant Victor Plumey, it housed Metzger's Dry Goods, one of the first East Side businesses, which was family operated for well over 100 years. Many Civil War veterans are seen here, as the Plumey Block was an early meeting place for the Ford Post, Grand Army of the Republic. It later became known as the Garbe Block, and on its site is now a Wendy's restaurant. *Submitted by Mary Liebherr.*

HOLD ON TO YOUR HAT.

Students of the old Franklin Elementary School are posed on the front steps in this 1885 photograph. (Notice the children in the front row all holding their decorated hats). Franklin was the first permanent large brick school in East Toledo, built in 1871. After several additions, a new school was constructed in 1924. The Board of Education closed the school in 2006, 135 years after the first school opened. *Submitted by Mary Liebherr.*

A HOME FOR THE PARENTLESS CHILD.

This circa 1862 photograph shows the Lutheran Orphans Home, or *Waisenhaus*, soon after it was built in 1860. In that era, when life expectancy was much shorter, many children lost both parents at a young age. Founded by Johannes Doerfler, who also organized First St. John Lutheran Church a year later, this early orphanage provided exceptional care for children over several generations. This first building stood on Seaman Road near Wheeling in East Toledo. Later, when the larger brick orphanage (still standing) was built, this building was enlarged to become the first *Altenheim*, or old folks home. The Lutheran Home Society, which still provides a variety of care facilities for older people, remains at this site, the second oldest Lutheran organization of its kind in the nation. *Submitted by Pastor Gerald H. Labuhn.*

GIVING THEIR REGARDS TO BROADWAY.

The Broadway View bar at 789 Broadway near Orchard was owned by Frederick Bussdieker in the 1880s and 1890s, when Broadway was still a gravel road and Orchard Street was still an orchard. It is likely that the gentleman in front of the bar leaning on the hitching post is Mr. Bussdieker. (Note the water pump between the two men at the left). His family lived above the establishment. *Submitted by Mary Good, great-granddaughter of Frederick Bussdieker.*

Toledo-Lucas County Public Library
Images In Time

the largest on-line searchable collection of photographs in Northwest Ohio.

In 1993, the Toledo-Lucas County Public Library undertook the awesome task of making its extensive collection of photographs available free to the public on-line. Approximately 80,000 images are now available through Images In Time.

The pictures range from the 1870s to present day, with the bulk taken between 1880 and World War II. The majority of the photographs depict scenes in the city of Toledo, although much of Northwestern Ohio and Southeastern Michigan are represented. Photographs depict the downtown area, with a large number of Toledo area industries (Jeep, Toledo Scale, Libbey Glass, Owens-Illinois, Libby-Owens-Ford, etc.), schools, hospitals, and parks represented as well.

Images In Time provides visitors to the Web site the opportunity to search the database by house address or street name, or by a subject or keyword.

Toledo-Lucas County Public LIBRARY

toledolibrary.org
419.259.5207

BIRTHPLACE OF HARVARD ELEMENTARY.

Albert Daske, a mason and lumberman (inset photo with his wife), built this large farmhouse about 1880 at what was then listed as 735 River Road. The house, with this scenic location overlooking the river, had a long stairway leading up to the front porch. It was the first one in this hilly ravine area just south of the Broadway and Glendale neighborhood. The house is near the site of Harvard Elementary School. *Submitted by Mary Good.*

OFF BROADWAY.

This impressive wooden building, the Liberty Theatre, stood at Avondale and Detroit Avenue surrounded by open fields circa 1899. It was a surprisingly large theater for the Vaudeville days and that location. Mt. Nebo Church stands on the site today. *Submitted by Corrine Gauthier.*

MARCHING OFF TO WAR.

A military band is marching near the Oliver House in 1898, as soldiers prepare to leave for the Spanish-American War. William Oechsler, an accountant at Schneck Coal Company who lived at 327 Oliver Street, took a whole series of historic photographs between 1898 and 1900. *Submitted by Robert Schaefer.*

SOLDIERS GETTING READY.

In a rare photo taken by William Oechsler in April 1898, soldiers are making preparations at the Lucas County Armory on Spielbusch Avenue near Cherry Street. The men are getting ready to march down Cherry to Summit Streets, and then down Summit to the train station where they would leave to fight in the Spanish-American War. *Submitted by Robert Schaefer.*

FROM MAILMAN TO PRESIDENT.

Only one of these two gentlemen walking north on Summit Street toward Walnut is really a letter carrier. On the left is mail carrier Fred Bruggemeier, who worked at the main post office at the time of this photo in 1895. On the right is said to be William Howard Taft, then a federal circuit court judge, who was elected our 27th President in 1908. The face and moustache certainly appear to be that of the future President. He was in town for a funeral and, being a friend of the Bruggemeier family, posed for this photograph. *Submitted by Kathy Beavers-Deck.*

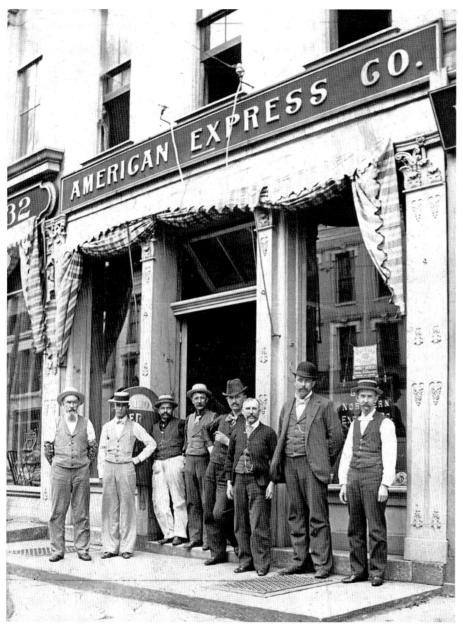

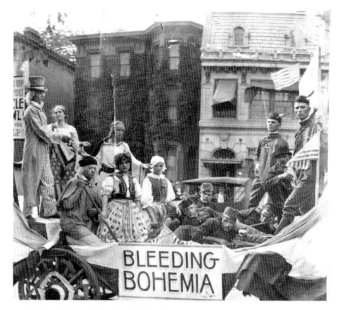

TROUBLE IN BOHEMIA.
The plight of Bohemia is the theme of this parade float, and the help of "Uncle Sam" is being sought. John Jiskra is at the left and Katrina Jiskra, second from left, in this World War I era photograph. Mr. Jiskra was a member of Suko Hall, an organization that promoted Hungarian causes. *Submitted by Jennifer Wherry.*

READY FOR BUSINESS.
The American Express Company started in 1850 as a hazardous messenger service, a desperately needed service as the West was expanding. They earned a reputation as the best source for delivering parcels and transporting cash and valuables. This American Express office stood at 72 Summit St. in 1887. In the 1920s, the office moved to 228 Summit St. *Submitted by Etta (Edelman) Hoot.*

ROLLING ON THE RIVER.

The *Pastime* is seen here steaming down the river with its big wheel rolling, taking hundreds of passengers off for a day of leisure. Known as the "Pride of Toledo" as early as the 1880s, the *Pastime* sailed to amusement parks such as Belle Isle or Presque Isle. In this vintage photograph, it is approaching the old Cherry Street Bridge with what is now International Park in the background. (The passengers in the stern seem unfazed by the black smoke pouring from the stack). *Submitted by Connie Warner and Harold Mucci.*

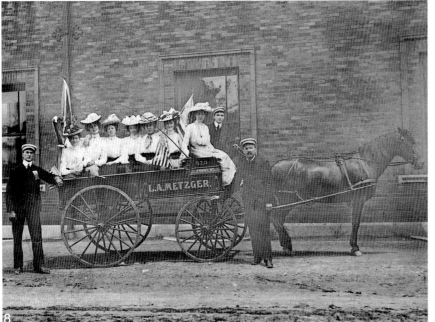

ROOM FOR ONE MORE?

The occasion is unknown, but these ladies are all dressed up to celebrate as they pose in L. A. Metzger's wagon circa 1900. The little horse, however, may well be glad to have a rest while this picture is taken, probably beside the Plumey Block along Main Street. Louis Metzger was in the California gold rush of 1849 and, when he returned to Toledo, joined in business with the Plumey family in a dry goods store at Front and Main Streets in East Toledo. The Metzger family home, built in 1867, still stands at Sixth Street and Euclid Avenue. *Submitted by Mary Liebherr.*

Reeb
FUNERAL HOME

For nearly 90 years, Reeb Funeral Home has been conducting business with residents of Northwest Ohio. We have been the choice of thousands of families in their time of need, and have worked diligently to offer caring service at fair prices.

Reeb Funeral Home remains independently owned, operated, and committed, to the same philosophies the business was built on generations ago.

5712 N. Main Street • Sylvania, Ohio
419-882-2033

THROUGH RAIN AND SNOW.
U. S. Post Office Station B was at 3031 Monroe Street in Auburndale when this photo was taken about 1905. The station closed about 1926. Pictured here (from left to right) are letter carriers Benjamin F. Sower, Lyman C. Mason, George W. Yost, Ernest E. Turney, Superintendent Jasper William Munson, John Vernier, Charles A. Coe and Charles J. Winkler. *Submitted by John Connors.*

ALL HAIL KING WAMBA!
In the summer of 1908, Toledo had hosted the Civil War veterans from all over the country in a huge patriotic celebration. The following year, with the hope of perpetuating some kind of Mardi Gras-type tradition, the Wamba Festival was invented. Here, the Toledo Newsboys Band is marching down Superior Street in the Wamba Festival parade in August 1909. A king and queen were crowned, and all kinds of parades and festivities took place in this unique civic extravaganza. What was meant to be an annual event died after its only year of existence, but interesting photos such as this keep the memory of the Wamba Festival alive. *Submitted by Fred Okun.*

BRING IT ON.
Not many smiles on this group, but that's because they played serious football. Until Scott and Waite high schools were built (in another 10 years), Toledo satisfied its football passion with a conglomerate team called the Toledo Maroons. The Maroons were known for defeating regional championship teams from around Ohio and Michigan quite regularly by scores of 40-0 and 48-0. These 1905 players look too clean to have played already; Armory Park at Canton and Spielbusch Avenues was the most popular site for football games, in spite of its tendency to become a mud pit. The Lucas County Armory (background, left) was the sports/entertainment complex of its day. Billy Sunday preached there and Bing Crosby sang there as one of the Rhythm Boys, backed by the Paul Whiteman Orchestra. *Submitted by Fred Okun.*

WORLD-CLASS MEATS.

Kurtz Meat Market was a mainstay of downtown Toledo since Jacob Kurtz put his name over the door in 1861. Its meat-cutting standards were exceptional, and in 1923 the company started the National School of Meat Cutting. The school attracted students from all over the world, occupied three downtown buildings and offered a six-week course developed by the elite Culinary Institute of America in Hyde Park, New York. In this 1905 photo, Kurtz Meat Market stood at 514 Adams St. John McGrath stands behind the counter, third from left, ready to serve the next customer. *Submitted by Sally Saba, granddaughter of John McGrath.*

THE CLIP-CLOP STOP.

At the turn of the century, horse-drawn carriages and trucks were still the predominant mode of transportation. The area in and around downtown Toledo was dotted with liveries and blacksmith services like this one owned by Charles Zimmerman at 204 Hamilton Street. *Submitted by Fred Okun.*

ONGOING PROJECT.
In 1908 the steamer *Yuma*, loaded with flaxseed, tore from its moorings and crashed into the west end of the old Cherry Street Bridge. A temporary span was constructed with many wooden supports, as seen in this ground-level photograph, until the new bridge could be completed in 1914. Undamaged sections of the old metal bridge were floated downriver to become the Ash-Consaul Bridge, which lasted until 1957. *Submitted by Sue Ricci.*

LAST OF THE CHIPPEWA TRIBE.
Victoria Cadaract (seated), shown here with a cousin from Walpole Island, was the last living full-blooded Native American in Ottawa County until her death in 1915. She was born near Ironville in East Toledo; her grandfather was a Chippewa chief. Her father died when she was young, and her mother remarried to a brother of Peter Navarre. Her own husband (of half French decent) also died young, leaving her two children. She wove and sold baskets for a living, walking eight miles to East Toledo or three miles to Curtice for supplies. She lived in a cabin near what is now the entrance to Chippewa Golf Course on SR 579. The course, opened in 1927, was named for her. *Submitted by James Blum.*

STATE HOSPITAL GROUNDS.
A lady in white, perhaps a nurse, stands at the corner of the Women's Hospital on the State Hospital grounds about 1912. The Renaissance-style stone building with its scrolled gable ends and massive chimneys was located by the large pond near Detroit Avenue toward Glendale, part of the extensive hospital campus. *Submitted by Sharon Yaros.*

TIME FOR SOME FUN.

The Scenic stood on Broadway in Walbridge Park at the beginning of the 20th century. It was called a casino, which at the time meant an entertainment hall consisting of concession stands, a photography booth, fruit stands and probably an early nickelodeon theater. It attracted visitors entering the park as they got off the streetcars. Nearby stood a figure-eight roller coaster and other amusement rides. At the time of this photo in 1907, the Zoo across the street had merely a few cages of animals; Walbridge Park was the main destination for visitors. The Scenic did not last very long, though, as park operators thought it took up room that could be better used for rides and other more exciting forms of entertainment. It was razed shortly after this picture was taken. *Submitted by Connie Warner and Harold Mucci.*

IT'S A GRAND OLD FLAG.

This rare 1908 photo of the famous Grand Army of the Republic living flag shows it from ground level. Every year GAR veterans of the Civil War chose a city for their national encampment, and in 1908 it was Toledo's turn. As part of the huge celebration, a living flag was made up of hundreds of schoolchildren in bleachers at Toledo Spain Plaza at Collingwood Boulevard and Jefferson Avenue. The children wore red, white and blue clothing to form the flag as they sang patriotic songs. They were also taught to sway to the music at different times to give the appearance of the flag waving in the breeze. *Submitted by Sue Ricci.*

ALLEY-OOP.
Bowling was highly popular in Toledo and elsewhere in the early 1900s. In 1908, in the East Side's Birmingham neighborhood, bowlers frequented John Monoky's three-lane wooden bowling alley on Whittemore Street near Genesee. After the building burned to the ground, Mr. Monoky rebuilt and opened a saloon in 1924. While working at the bar and the Monoky Cafe (an East Toledo favorite) that succeeded it, his son John "Johnny Monk" Monoky, Jr., fed his appetite for bowling. He earned national renown on the traveling team circuit, won numerous state tournaments, and was inducted into the Toledo Bowling Hall of Fame in 1978. *Submitted by Robert Fiddler.*

SUNNY DAY AT THE OLD CORNER STORE.
This early convenience store stood at the corner of Erie and Suder Streets when this picture was taken by Cloyd Mills in 1909. Along with ice cream, it advertises milk, bread, cake and candy. Resting on the porch is Agnes Taynor with some of her children, perhaps taking a respite from the hot summer sun. *Submitted by Ken Mills, grandson of Cloyd Mills.*

DICK, JIM AND BARNEY.
Dick, Jim and Barney, driven by Engineer Charles M. Harrison, draw a Toledo Fire Department steamer past John Goldbach's drug store on Jefferson Avenue, crossing Erie Street. The apparatus was a La France "boiler on wheels" with a pump capacity of 1350 gallons per minute on five lines of hose. The entire unit, which also carried some coal, weighed eight tons, requiring the three-horse team. Engineer Harrison served as a member of the department from 1899 until 1918 and was stationed at Number 3 Engine House, located at Jefferson and Ontario streets, when this photograph was taken by John H. Nort in 1908. The last run by horse-drawn equipment in Toledo was made in August 12, 1916 from Station Number 15 at Airline Avenue and Gibbons Street. The equipment seen here was later converted to a motor-driven wagon as shown in *Toledo: Our Life, Our Times, Our Town, Volume I* (pages 60 and 61). *Submitted by Philip R. Harrison, great-grandson of Charles M. Harrison.*

BEAUTIES AND THE BEACH.
Louise Meyer (top right, head down) and her group of co-workers from a local sewing factory in 1910 get a refreshing break from the oppressive heat at Toledo Beach. In the days before air conditioning and public swimming pools, places like Toledo Beach were very popular. Until the Roaring 20s, properly dressed women covered everything between the neck and ankles, except when "bathing" at the beach, even during muggy Maumee Valley summers. *Submitted by Judy (Jokinen) Nickoloff, niece of Louise Meyer.*

WORTH THE "WAITE".
The Henry J. Spieker Company is making preparations for what is believed to be the construction of Waite High School in this circa 1910 photo. The old Duck Creek ravine ran through the lower part of the property on which Waite was built. In this photograph the trees in the background may be those along the creek. Helping to move dirt on the site is Harry Oman, seated in the wagon with the dark horses. Harry is the grandfather of Jean Glenn. Waite High School took about six years to build because of a shortage of men and materials during World War I, opening for classes in September of 1914. *Submitted by Glen Torrence.*

IN LIKE A LION.
The 1910 Maumee River spring thaw caused massive damage as ice 15 inches or more thick jammed along the waterway. Unusually high rains and ice blockages caused floods, carrying massive slabs of ice that damaged bridges, tore up and twisted entire sections of railroad tracks, and destroyed headstones in Maumee Cemetery. It wasn't all bad: nearby farmers collected baskets of fish in puddles left behind in the fields. One Toledo man retrieved two carp totaling 43 pounds. *Submitted by Louis Boehk.*

THE LATEST MODEL.
Willys-Overland workers gather around new 1910 Model 38 motor cars assembled at their factory on West Central near Yost. The young man whose face is seen just above the hand around the steering wheel on the left is Elvin C. Myers at age 18. The Model 38 was the Toledo Fire Department's first motor car, driven by Chief William Mayo out of headquarters at Engine House No. 3. *Submitted by El Myers, son of Elvin C. Myers.*

EAT, DRINK AND BE MERRY.
These ladies are certainly not afraid of sea sickness as they enjoy a trip on one of the many lake steamers that sailed from Toledo in the early 1900s. In the photograph are Delilah, center, (who later married Frank Wirebaugh) and two of her friends, Kathryn, left, and Lillah, right, on a trip to Put-in-Bay about 1910. Frank Wirebaugh was a civil engineer for the city of Toledo who worked on many projects, including the Cherry Street Bridge. *Submitted by Jeffrey Wirebaugh, grandson of Frank and Delilah Wirebaugh.*

IT'S RAINING KIDS!
In 1912, Cloyd Mills took this photograph of the drainage ditch across from 1862 Chase Street filled with rainwater and neighborhood children: (from left) An unidentified girl, Carl Cox, Florence Zink, Lavern Mills, Irma Mills, Louise Elkost, Teresa Lefave, Rosetta Davis, Alice Hamann, Clarence Schupp, Zelma Schupp, Alfred Hamann, Alta Elkost, an unknown toddler, Jeff Irwin, an unknown boy, Walter Brimmer, Nelly Irwin, Jack Irwin and another unidentified girl. (Lavern "Vern" Mills, who supplied these names, is 100 years old this year). *Submitted by Lavern Mills and son Ken Mills.*

VALET BICYCLE PARKING?

These two young men have parked their bicycles in front of Edgar A. Kopf's general repair shop, even though they seem to be in fine working order. (Notice the tracks running down the street at the time of this photograph, which appears to be circa 1910). *Submitted by Lou Boehk.*

ROUGHING IT.

Charlotte "Hattie" Thetford and her son, William Edward Thetford, create the perfect camp July 5, 1910. Hattie's camp includes all the comforts of home: a wicker rocker, a dinner table and chairs with china and linens. Unseen in this photo in the interior of the tent: a mirror, rug on the floor, a bird in a cage, a living room chair and candelabra. And what camping trip would be complete without the family pooch, chickens and a goat? *Submitted by Delbert Schwab, grandson of Hattie and son of William.*

NAVAL TRAINING SHIP.

The *U.S.S. Essex* (III) served as a training vessel for the Ohio Naval Militia in Toledo from 1904 to 1916. Previously decommissioned, it was brought to Toledo and refurbished, nearly colliding with an ocean liner en route. The *Essex* gave a much-needed boost to the all-volunteer unit, which has served Ohio since 1896 as the naval arm of the Ohio Adjutant General's Department. The current Ohio Naval Militia headquarters is on the Camp Perry Training Site. *Submitted by Harold Mucci and daughter Connie Warner.*

A FAMILY TRADITION.

The players intently taking aim in this photo are the 1912-1913 St. John University basketball team. Second from right is Leo S. Hillebrand, whose uncle, Carl Hillebrand, donated the woodchuck that became the first animal at the Toledo Zoo in 1899. St. John College opened in 1898 on Superior Street. In 1903 it became known as St. John University, consisting of a four-year academy (high school) as well as a four-year bachelor of arts college. The basketball team played in the gymnasium of the nearby Westminster Church, and during that 1912-1913 season played games against Ohio State and Notre Dame. St. John University closed in 1936, a victim of the depression, but St. John's High School was established in 1965. *Submitted by Carol Arnold and Nancy Ligibel.*

SKILLED GLASS WORKERS.

In 1888, Edward Drummond Libbey moved his glassmaking operations to Toledo, where the skilled glass workers of the Lefevre family found worthy employment in 1902. Henri Lefevre had earned *maitre verrier travilleur* (master glass worker) status at the Val St. Lambert Glass Works in Belgium. (Founded in 1825, its early shareholders included King Guillame I.) Henri was a gaffer; son Leon a skilled off-hand worker; and sons Nestor and Gaston were glassblowers. Pictured here are the American Flint Glass Workers, Local 19 members, from the Libbey Glass Factory A, outside the hall above Kruse's Saloon at Buffalo and Michigan streets after a union meeting in 1912. Leon Lefevre is fourth from left. *Submitted by Robert Gaston Lefevre, son of Gaston.*

NOT RUSH HOUR.
This view of Main Street in Bowling Green in 1912 is a vintage street scene from the turn of the last century. The utility poles with many cross bars are typical of about 1900, as are the many awnings, brick pavement and single streetcar track down the middle of the road. Also, there are still buggies on the street, and the building at the far left has an "Old West" false front. *Submitted by Sharon Yaros.*

RAPIDLY RISING.
Easter Week in 1913 brought several days of heavy rains. On March 25, Ohio's rivers overflowed, causing the worst day of flooding in Ohio history with hundreds of deaths in riverfront towns. One of those towns was Grand Rapids. Here, residents with canoes appear to be bringing townspeople to higher ground. The town remained flooded for a week, with water as high as eight feet in some buildings. *Submitted by Etta (Edelman) Hoot.*

GREAT GATHERING.

In 1915, Toledoans lined the streets to watch the Grand Army of the Republic (GAR) march past. Formed by Union Army veterans of the Civil War, the GAR helped reunite the nation, aided veterans in getting their pensions and provided for the families of fallen comrades. Seven years before, the national GAR held its annual encampment in Toledo. The city had to provide tents for many; there wasn't enough lodging available for the estimated 100,000 Civil War veterans who attended. It was called "the greatest gathering to ever assemble in Toledo." *Submitted by Ronald Gabel, Toledo Yacht Club historian.*

ENTER THE MOTORIZED AGE.

By 1914, cities like Toledo were responding faster with vehicles like this one, parked on Superior Street opposite the old central police station. Toledo's pioneer automobile patrol squad is, from left, Sgt. Guy Tribbels; Roy Dietz, a civilian instructor; Paul Wiesenberg, later a fingerprint expert in Toledo's Bureau of Identification; Harry Jennings, named police chief in 1922; William Schultz; Carl Hollinger; Fred Pawlicki and William Myers. (The drivers identity is unknown). *Submitted by Nancy Stover, granddaughter of 42-year veteran police officer William H. Stover and daughter of TPD officer William P. Stover.*

TIME FOR SCHOOL.
Young Adrian Lisiakowski, a student at St. Stanislas School, poses proudly with his special schoolbag in 1916. Years later he felt compelled to conceal his Polish heritage, by changing his name to Lendecker, to get a job with the New York Central Railroad. He got the job as a machinist at the Roundhouse on Fearing Boulevard and went on to build airstrips on Iwo Jima and retire from the railroad. *Submitted by Dolores (Lendecker) Slowinski, daughter of Adrian Lendecker.*

A LOT TO CELEBRATE.
Workers at Willys-Overland Motor Company in Toledo assemble for a photo and, perhaps, a performance at the former Pope-Toledo automotive plant. The man left of the tuba player (center) is Otto Krueger. By 1912, Willys-Overland had become America's second-largest producer of cars, behind only Ford. The Overland Model 38 was the first to be built in Toledo. *Submitted by Dorothy Michael, great-niece of Otto Krueger.*

LOCAL BREWER'S HOTEL.

Edward Radbone, Jr., superintendent of Forest Cemetery and vice-president of Finlay Brewing, built the Radbone Hotel where the Wabash & Erie Canal intersected Summit Street at the turn of the century. (The old canal bed is at the right.) The hotel, of course, had a large saloon; Mr. Radbone anticipated many hotel guests during the Ohio Centennial Exposition, but the festivities were moved to Chillicothe. Business was brisk later on, however, when casino and bootlegger activity was at its peak along the Maumee Bay shoreline in the '20s. *Submitted by Lois (Holtz) Horner and Sarah Horner, granddaughter and great-granddaughter of Ned Radbone.*

TRAMPLING DEMON RUM.

Harry Oman, his son Kennard, and two fine horses are prepared for a Prohibition parade in 1918. On the float, Miss Ohio is pushing Ohio voters to flatten the evil influence of "booze." Whether a real "Miss Ohio" participated in the parade is unknown. *Submitted by Glen Torrence.*

WANNA RACE?

Fredrick Vincent Kunz owned this garage at 1735 Broadway near Prouty about 1916. He is pictured at the upper right with many of his friends and some fine vintage vehicles, perhaps early Pope roadsters made in Toledo. The young men are dressed in a variety of riding fashions of that early automotive era. *Submitted by Rick Kunz.*

THIS WAY TO SAFETY.

Freighters entering the Maumee River from Lake Erie had plenty of hazards to avoid, especially in the dark of night. A single beacon on Turtle Island proved inadequate. To improve Toledo's prospects as a port city, installation of a series of Maumee Bay Range Lights began with this main Cribb Light in 1884 – the only significant improvement to navigation of the Maumee River channel. After larger freighters collided with them more than once, the fixed lantern Cribb Lights were deemed hazards and removed in the 1950s. *Submitted by Ronald Gabel and the Western Lake Erie Historical Society.*

GIBBS HOME ON RAMBO LANE.
Percy Phillip Gibbs, his wife and daughter, emigrated from Birmingham, England in 1919. He purchased land on the former Ketcham horse farm at 5539 Rambo Lane. He built his house from the ground up, using lumber from the Ketcham barns. After laying the foundation, he posed for this photograph. On the back of the photo he wrote, "How do you like my wooden hut that keeps your ears warm?" The house is a 22 ft. x 24 ft. one-floor bungalow with four rooms. An addition and porches were added later. In 1920, a son, Kenneth, was born in the house. The Gibbs home remained in the family until the late 1960s. *Submitted by Kenneth P. Gibbs.*

JACK THE GIANT FELLER.
Little is known about this photo of William "Jack" Dempsey, left, with Evelyn (Hurlbut) Venzke, age 6, and her stepfather, Everett. It appears to have been taken at the stadium or training camp built at Bay View Park especially for the crowds expected for the now famous Dempsey-Willard boxing match July 4, 1919. In spite of the 100-degree heat, 20,000 attended. While training, Mr. Dempsey lived at 2465 Parkwood Ave., and he returned to Toledo many times. *Submitted by David Venzke, son of Evelyn.*

READY TO RIDE.
Joseph Pollauf stands in front of a shop selling Excelsior "Auto-Cycles" in this 1920s photograph. In 1905, Excelsior built its first single-speed, single-cylinder motorcycle in Chicago, Illinois. In 1927, Andrew Pollauf owned a motorcycle shop at 2011 Starr Avenue, probably the location of this picture. Young Joseph appears to be all set to ride one of the bikes. *Submitted by Connie Calmes.*

THE HEIGHT OF FASHION.
A young cashier with bobbed hair is waiting to help a lady dressed in the most fashionable 1920s attire at B.R. Baker's Summit Street store. Baker's was located at 435-439 Summit Street from the 1890s until opening their new store at Adams and Superior Streets in 1930. (Note the vintage telephone on the counter and the gentleman at the far right, probably waiting to open the door for the lady). *Submitted by Dolores Eberly.*

DOG-POWERED AUTOMOBILE?

Christine and Don McColl are cruising along in their homemade gas-driven car with flywheel in this delightful 1920 photograph. In the background is the new Wildwood Addition and the interurban line railroad tracks. *Submitted by Beverly McCarthy and Roger VanGunten.*

WHEN THE TRAIL WAS A CANAL.

An early model car is crossing the Glendale Avenue swing bridge over the canal in South Toledo in this 1921 photograph. One of many important WPA projects of the Depression era was the draining of the canal and the building of the Anthony Wayne Trail along its route. Stones from the canal were used in other projects, including many of the buildings at the Toledo Zoo. *Submitted by Beverly McCarthy and Roger VanGunten.*

Banner
MATTRESS & FURNITURE CO.

Providing Banner Days and Better Nights

for more than 78 years

Since 1927, Toledo's been our home for manufacturing the most comfortable mattresses in the world.

Because we have the home advantage, a great work force, and local show rooms, we're able to provide exemplary service and significant savings to our customers. Besides its line of Toledo made Banner Comfort Bedding, Banner Mattress has the largest furniture inventory in Northwest Ohio. We can also custom fabricate mattresses to meet your special needs.

Being in the neighborhood makes it easy for us to deliver comfort directly to your home six days a week!

Circa 1965 Monroe Street

Locally owned and operated to serve you!

3342 Monroe Street
419.244.3751

6004 Hill Avenue
419.865.6164

2521 West Alexis
419.472.0220

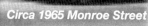
3249 Navarre Ave.
419.693-5955

THIS BOAT WON'T FLOAT.
Sometime before 1920, Edward "Ned" Radbone bought this former houseboat, *The Defender*, and placed it on land he leased from the McLeary family at McLeary's Point on the Ottawa River, known then as Ten Mile Creek. He and his family lived there every summer, raising carp in two ponds, and made a decent living selling them to New York fishmongers. *Submitted by Lois (Holtz) Horner and Sarah Horner, granddaughter and great-granddaughter of Ned Radbone.*

LEAVING THE POINT.
During the Civil War, Louis Zistel used his boats to transport Confederate prisoners to a jail on Johnson's Island. In 1870, he used them to bring vacationers to his small beer garden, bathhouse and dance floor on the peninsula called Cedar Point. By 1929, around the time of this photo, Cedar Point had introduced its second roller coaster, the Cedar Point Cyclone, creating a new right of passage for young teens like Vivian Werner (left) and her older sister, Virginia. (No one is quite sure of the gentleman's identity or the source of the sign at lower left.) *Submitted by Carol Arnold, daughter of Vivian (Criqui) Werner.*

WHERE'S THE FIRE?
The first motorized fire truck at Engine House No. 5 is seen here in this circa 1920s photograph after it crashed onto the lawn of the Foth Funeral Home at City Park and Nebraska Avenue. Fred Bussdieker said the firemen were not used to the speed of the new engine and took the turn too fast. The next thing they knew they were in the flower bed of the funeral home, attracting quite a large crowd and more excitement than usual at a mortuary. The Foth Funeral Home still exists today as Foth-Dorfmeyer on Sylvania Avenue at Woodley. *Submitted by Mary Good, granddaughter of Fred Bussdieker.*

FLYING HIGH.
Those magnificent men in their flying machine! Lieutenant Louis Rutter, his cousin Hiram Olderman and Louis's grandfather pose for a photo at Cedar Point during the roaring and soaring 1920s. Cedar Point is now considered the second oldest amusement park in North America. The first roller coaster was introduced there in 1892. *Submitted by Tom Rutter.*

STRIKE UP THE BAND.
This fine-looking group of musicians represented Branch 100 of the National Association of Letter Carriers, Toledo, Ohio. They are standing on the steps of the new Main Post Office, built in 1910 and known for its classical architecture, at 1300 Jefferson Avenue in this 1923 photograph. *Submitted by Connie Niese.*

FIVE MEN AND A HORSE.
Engine House No. 5 must have still employed at least one horse in this 1920s photograph. The station was at the corner of Broadway and Emerald Streets near the I-75 overpass. The Coyle Funeral Home was on the corner across Emerald Street. The fire house, with its large Italianate window hoods, dates from the 1880s or earlier. At the left, Fred Bussdieker, known for his sense of humor, strikes a whimsical pose. *Submitted by Mary Good, granddaughter of Fred Bussdieker.*

LAYING THE CORNERSTONE.
Reverend Ryan posed next to the cornerstone of Somerset United Brethren Church in this 1922 photograph. At the right end of the first row is Rev. Powell, and in the second row over Rev. Ryan's right shoulder is Rev. Bollenger. Next to Rev. Bollenger, left to right, is Mr. Klotz and Mr. Sampsell. The church was located at 2025 Wayne Street, and it later merged with Western Avenue Methodist to become New Hope Methodist Church. *Submitted by Marilee Taylor, archivist of New Hope United Methodist.*

SECRETS ON THE STREET.
Scintillating stories have always been hot sellers, as Morris Hirsch (right, standing) and Eddie Weineman (seated) knew well. In this New Year's Day 1925 photo, the unidentified gentleman has just delivered the new issue of Secrets magazine to Mr. Hirsch's newsstand in front of the S. S. Kresge store on Summit Street, directly across from the Toledo Trust Building (background). The driver worked for Hirsch News Agency, a magazine wholesale business also owned by Mr. Hirsch. Despite the weather (the temperature was below zero on this morning), he ran this outdoor newsstand from 1911 until 1941. *Submitted by Gordon Hirsch, son of Morris Hirsch.*

FRESH-FACED FUTURE.
Little Jeanette Thomas was five years old here in 1923. Magdelena (Wernert) Thomas, Jeanette's great-great-grandmother, lived nearby on one of several tracts of land owned by the Wernert family. In the background is the J. E. Wernert grocery store on Douglas and Tremainsville roads in the area called Wernerts Corners. *Submitted by Judy (Lebowsky) Shook, daughter of Jeanette (Thomas) Lebowsky.*

RETREAT FROM THE HEAT.
Joe Thomas, far right, and friends take a break from the heat at Mr. Thomas's cottage in Point Place. Mr. Thomas owned the truck and its business – *Gray's Home Made Mayonnaise & Sandwich Spread* – on Locust Street. The men in their handsome bathing duds (in the 1920s, when this was taken, swimming was called "bathing") are, from left, an unidentified man and friends Alphonse "Al" Mlotzek and Bernard "Bernie Gressler". *Submitted by Judy (Lebowsky) Shook, granddaughter of Joe Thomas.*

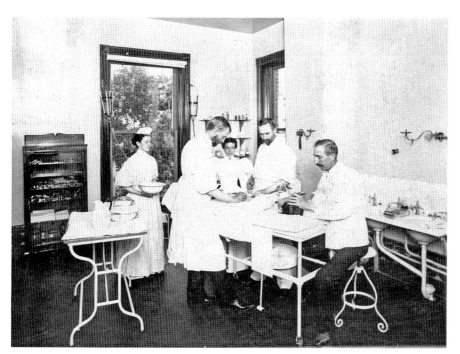

AHEAD OF HIS TIME.
In 1900, physicians still scoffed at the idea of sterilizing surgical tools or even hand-washing before treating patients. Toledo surgeon William J. Gillette, M.D., was ahead of his time. Although the use of surgical masks, gloves and clothing covers is not yet in evidence here, Dr. Gillette (second from left) was one of the first in the region to institute these practices in his clinic at Robinwood Avenue and Virginia Street in 1898. The 50-bed Robinwood Hospital took its place in 1906. It was renamed St. Luke's in 1951 and soon relocated for expansion to the City of Maumee. *Submitted by St. Luke's Hospital.*

FRESH FROM THE FARMS.
In Toledo, the precursor to the supermarket was the indoor market at Summit and Cherry Streets. Families found a vast variety of fruits and vegetables here, as well as homemade ice cream and modern amenities like electric lights suspended low enough to give customers plenty of light to examine the goods. When this photo was taken in 1922, John McGrath had his own stand here. *Submitted by Sally Saba, granddaughter of John McGrath.*

SHOWING THEIR STRIPES.

The Woodward Technical High School football team is shown here in 1923. The location of the photo is uncertain, but perhaps was taken at the school, which stood at Michigan and Adams Streets where the Main Library is today. When Scott and Waite opened in 1913 and 1914, respectively, the old Central High School downtown became a manual training school for younger students. They added a high school curriculum in 1919, and by the early 1920s had as many as 400 students. It was named after Calvin Woodward, a noted leader in manual training schools in St. Louis. A larger building was soon needed, and Woodward High School was opened in 1928. *Submitted by Tom Rutter.*

ANCHORS AWEIGH!

With all his tools lined up behind him, Ewald Sieler, Sr., stands at his work bench at the Toledo Shipbuilding Company, later American Shipbuilding, on Front Street in this March 17, 1923 photograph. Mr. Sieler was a pattern maker who was known for designing the anchor for the *Mackinaw*. *Submitted by Joanne Clark, daughter of Ewald Sieler, Sr.*

"YOU CALL, WE HAUL."

That is the motto of E.J. Braatz & Son Moving and Storage Company, whose moving van is seen here about 1925 in front of White Trucks Sales and Service. All the salesmen and workers, along with three ladies behind them, are lined up to work at The White Company at 1811-1815 Jefferson Avenue. The E.J. Braatz Company was at 630 Huron Street. Fifth from the left, in this photo, is Charles Holderman, who, with his brother Fred, had an auto repair shop at 2224-2232 Jefferson Avenue, where Mercy Hospital was later built. *Submitted by Sandra Drake, granddaughter of Charles Holderman, and Judith Holman.*

STOP THAT TROLLEY!
Drivers and mechanics for the Community Traction Company take time out for this company photo circa 1925. This barn was on Starr Avenue near Raymer. Drivers would play cards out front between shifts. Community Traction Company was the predecessor to TARTA (Toledo Area Regional Transit Authority). *Submitted by Jeanne Belding.*

AN INDUSTRIOUS YOUNG MAN.

Lloyd McCracken (center), 14, was already a fixture at C.R. Webster's market in 1925. The boy was 12, selling *Toledo Times* newspapers in front of the store at 3369 Maplewood Avenue at Castle Boulevard, when Mr. Webster (right) invited him inside to work. He worked evenings in the market until he graduated in 1930 from the brand new Woodward High School (Woodward Technical School on Adams Street until 1929). *Submitted by Lloyd McCracken.*

A DREAM COME TRUE.

Until Jonas Salk discovered the vaccine for polio in 1955, many children developed severe cases of the infection, often in infancy. William Riley's son James was little more than a year old in 1920 when he contracted polio, which left him with crippling injuries. By then Toledo's Rotary Club was well known for its services to these children. So in 1917, when Emma Roberts of the District Nurse Association dreamed of a school for physically challenged kids, she spoke with the Rotary Club. Previous president and local wholesale grocer Charles Feilbach led the campaign. Feilbach School opened behind Cherry School later that year. In 1925, Rotarians took Feilbach students to Walbridge Amusement Park for the day. Young James Riley (fifth from the right), age 6, was among them. Today, the school on Cass Road – Glendale-Feilbach Elementary – bears witness to his good works. *Submitted by James and Rosemary (McGarry) Riley.*

TOLEDO'S ONE AND ONLY.

Girl Scout Troop No. 2's drum and bugle corps – the only one in Toledo – poses for a photographer in May 1926 at the First Unitarian Church on Collingwood Boulevard at Bancroft Street. The corps, led by Scout Captain Mrs. James Vogle, Jr., includes buglers Cynthia Morgan, Marjorie Horan, Betty Williams, Dorothy Hall, Katherine Harsch, Martha Lancashire, Miriam Macomber, Merilee Highfill, Helen Henderson, Betty Alter, Caroline Dickey, Freda Johnson, Margaret Robbins and Oleva Edler. The drummers are Adelaide Morgan, Nettie Bell Thomas, Ruth Cartwright, Betty Everson, Vera Dickson, Janet Vallance, Betty Hill, Bertha Brown, Alice Williams and Lois Stickles. *Submitted by Beverly Miner and the archives of the Girl Scout Council of Maumee Valley.*

SPEEDY DELIVERY.

The E.H. Adkins Grocery Store at Monroe Street and Lawrence Avenue opened for business in 1920. The owner, Edwin Hays Adkins, is shown second from the right under a pair of roller skates. The skates were used to speed up grocery deliveries in 1927. *Submitted by D. Adkins.*

GOT MILK?
Page Dairy had a traveling baseball team for many years in Toledo, and this photo shows the team and batboy at an unknown field on July 24, 1927. The player fifth from the left is William Demlow. During in the 1920s, the diamond in East Toledo where the Weiler Homes now stand was known as Page Field. Also, 1927 was the year that Casey Stengel managed the Mud Hens to a championship at Swayne Field. (Notice the cars lined up in the background). *Submitted by Ron Born.*

ELEVEN WORKING, ONE NAPPING.
These workers pose to have their picture taken as they complete the South Avenue Bridge on August 12, 1927. Located near Highland Park and spanning Swan Creek, the bridge was recently rebuilt. (Look closely at the bottom of the pole in the lower left center of the photograph – you can just see the legs of someone who, we assume, is beating the August heat with a nap). Pictured fifth from the left is Onie Sugg. *Submitted by Gary Sugg, grandson of Onie, and Elizabeth and Anne-Marie Sugg, great-granddaughters of Onie.*

MILE HIGH.
Zeno Carl Wasserman and Nellie Mae (Walters) Wasserman are perched precariously on the old mile marker at the corner of Arlington (left) and Byrne Road or perhaps Detroit Avenue about 1927. Maumee Valley Hospital's working farm can be seen in the background. Mr. Wasserman chose a very clever way to get close to his pretty young lady. *Submitted by Mary Ann Wasserman.*

A DAY AT VOLLMAR PARK.

From its opening in 1900, Vollmar Park on state routes 65 and 582 was unique among Ohio's 50-plus amusement parks for its low-key, relaxed atmosphere. Vollmar Park offered everything from a bathing beach and carnival rides to ball games and a covered bridge ideal for romantic moments. Little wonder, then, that Bunting Brass & Bronze Company held its annual picnic there in July 1927, attended by many families including the Jacksons: Richard Jackson, 7 (front with bowtie), Betty (second to right of Richard), Tom (next to Betty), mother Blanche (back row, fifth from left) and uncle Art Jackson (eighth from left). Within 20 years, Bunting Brass & Bronze would become the largest bushing manufacturer in the world. *Submitted by Ken Jackson, son of Richard Jackson.*

Roy Walton, 1927

Howard Walton, 1935.

Ray Walton, 1928

FOOD FOR THOUGHT.

Ray, Roy and Howard Walton grew up in the food business. Their father, Carl, and his brother Harry, owned the Walton Brothers Bakery at 804 Dorr Street. Each of Carl's sons managed a Kroger Grocery & Baking Co. store: Roy in 1927, on Monroe Street between Superior and St. Clair streets (top left); Ray in 1928, on Nebraska Avenue at Erie Street (bottom right, center); and Howard in 1935, on Lawrence Avenue between Oakwood and Lincoln Avenues (outside the store). They all moved on to other jobs but stayed in the food business for life. *Submitted by David Walton, son of Roy Walton.*

STUCK IN THE MUD.
William and Clara Moritz wait for help on Brown Road with their Ford Model T in 1928. They were headed to St. John's Evangelical Lutheran Church on Seaman Road when they got stuck in the mud. St. John's was rebuilt in 1928 (it still stands), also the last year the Model T was assembled. Mr. Moritz's father, John Jakob Moritz, was one of the church's charter members and helped build the original church in 1861. The Moritzes farmed 80 acres at Brown and Stadium roads. *Submitted by Roy Moritz, son of William and Clara Moritz.*

READY TO ROLL.
Marjorie Graumlich (McQueary), Max Klug and Al Graumlich are all dressed up with someplace to go as they pose on a wagon, peddle car and trike in front of the Graumlich home on Willys Parkway in 1928. *Submitted by Al Graumlich.*

LOCAL GOLF PRO.
Harry Harris was a golf instructor in Brighton and Willingdon (and is rumored to have provided golf instruction for British royalty) in his native England. He arrived in the U.S. in 1911 where he married Emma Vincent. In this photo they are posing on the entrance steps at Inverness Country Club where Mr. Harris served as golf pro from 1912 to 1917. Later, he worked as golf instructor at Collins Park under the City Division of Parks, Boulevards and Recreation. *Submitted by Joseph LaJeunesse, great-nephew of Emma (Vincent) Harris.*

WHO YOU CALLIN' OLD?
These "veteran" baseball players are looking fit in this circa 1929 photograph, which appears to have been taken on the steps of the Safety Building downtown. Roy Kaspitske is the young mascot or ball boy. The catcher was Frank Mayo, who is standing behind the manager or umpire (dressed in the suit and tie). *Submitted by Robert Uhrman.*

COMPLETED IN UNDER A YEAR.
The University of Toledo campus along Bancroft Street was mostly mud and trees as University Hall was nearing completion in this circa 1929 photograph. University Hall, of collegiate gothic architecture, was the first academic building on the new campus when the university moved from its Scott Park location. At the far right, the old Field House can be seen. *Submitted by Joan Rumpf.*

MAIL GOES AIRBORNE.

After the air feats of World War I pilots, the post-war years – and the daring 1920s, in particular – were spent creating peacetime uses for flight. One of the most significant was mail delivery. Initially using military planes, the U.S. Postal Service put the airplanes to use moving mail faster from coast to coast and paved the way for commercial aviation. The mail service contracted with numerous "transcontinental" airports whose pilots flew visually, sighting rivers and railroads as their only means of staying on course. Most men and women whose names are synonymous with "barnstorming" and daring stunts, including Charles Lindbergh, were contract pilots.

John "Jack" Amidon and wife Lenora visited the Transcontinental Airport of Toledo before the official dedication in 1929, when 35,000 people are said to have come to watch stunt pilots perform. Toledo was an important stop on several airmail routes between Detroit and Chicago, Cleveland and St. Louis (Lindbergh's home base). *Submitted by Jeanny Amidon and Rick Bryan, daughter and son-in-law of Jack and Lenora Amidon.*

COMPANY PICNIC EXCURSION.

For nine years, the Lion Store held lavish annual employee picnics. Management closed the store for the day and employees paraded to the river, led by a 32-piece band. There they boarded the ship to Sugar Island, near Middle Bass Island, which had an amusement park, dance pavilion and beach. Sugar Island was one of many popular "sweetwater" bathing resorts in and around Lake Erie around the turn of the century. Another was Cedar Point. *Submitted by Etta (Edelman) Hoot.*

LION STORE GROCERS.

The Lion Store Honor Award for Sales went to the Grocery Department in May 1929, located in the store basement. Customers bought fancy groceries here, including caviar. Identities of only three staff members seen here are known: May Orwig (far left), Lion Store buyer Harry Bannister (fourth from left), and Charles Edelman (second from right). Mr. Edelman was hired by the Lion Dry Goods Company (as it was known then) in 1909 and worked there for 50 years. *Submitted by Etta (Edelman) Hoot.*

THE WHEELS OF PROGRESS.

Toledo was a fast-growing city at the turn of the century; its population tripled in just 30 years, from 81,000 in 1890 to over 240,000 in 1920. Public transportation was crucial. Horse-drawn trolleys gave way to electric streetcars with more capacity (like the one seen here) in 1892. The interurban railroad offered transit to outlying areas, from the casino in Point Place to the boardwalk at Cedar Point and as far as Ann Arbor, Michigan. John "Jack" Amidon was a streetcar conductor on the Broadway line for a time in 1928. He was working the Cherry Street line when Lenora Gilbert boarded his streetcar for Central Catholic High School. They married in 1930. *Submitted by Jeanny Amidon and Rick Bryan, daughter and son-in-law of Jack and Lenora Amidon.*

GIRL SCOUT RUNABOUT.
This truck came in very handy for local Girl Scout troops in the 1930s. Trips to Camp Libbey were certainly easier: the Girl Scouts bought 248 acres of land on the Maumee River near Defiance in 1935 with funds from Edward Drummond Libbey and other donors. Here it is seen outside the Toledo Museum of Art, organized by Mr. Libbey, who was president of the museum from 1901 to 1925. The truck was available the same year the nationally sanctioned Girl Scout cookie sales began. Coincidence? *Submitted by Beverly Miner and the archives of the Girl Scout Council of Maumee Valley.*

BUILDING A FUTURE COLLEGE.
This 1930 photograph shows the building of St. Claire Academy, now St. Claire Hall at Lourdes College. Franciscan Sisters from Rochester, Minnesota, came to the Toledo area in 1916 with a mission to teach. They purchased 89 acres in Sylvania and established a new providence. It grew rapidly, and in 1930 this beautiful academic building was constructed. Since then many other outstanding Spanish-style buildings have been added to the campus, and Lourdes College, independently incorporated in 1973, has become one of Toledo's fine institutions of higher education. *Submitted by Helene Sheets of Lourdes College.*

SHOP 'TIL THEY DROP.

These shoppers, mostly gentlemen, are perhaps looking for bargains in hats at the new B.R. Baker's at Adams and Superior Streets. This picture is of the grand opening of the new store in September 1930. The original B. R. Baker store began in partnership with L.E. Flory at Front and Main Streets in East Toledo in 1886. Two years later after the business prospered, Baker's moved downtown to Summit Street. *Submitted by Dolores Eberly.*

WE NEVER TIRE.

Linker Tire and Supply Company was located in this home-like brick building at 4504 Lewis Avenue. This picture was taken about 1930, showing Linker's late 1920s delivery sedan, which offered day and night service. The company also had an early AAA affiliation, no doubt doing a fine business in those days of frequent flat tires. *Submitted by Robert Schaefer.*

LET'S SKATE.
These skaters are enjoying some wintertime fun on the Maumee River in this 1930s photograph. In the background nearer the shoreline are wind racing sailboats. These were popular activities on the river, dating back to the horse and sled racers of the late 1800s. The only danger was getting too close to the shore, where industrial runoff would melt the ice. *Submitted by Denny Taylor.*

TAKE 'EM TO THE BRIDGE.
Construction began on the Anthony Wayne (High Level) Bridge October 1, 1929. Here, workers are preparing for the setting of concrete piles along Utah Street. The piles will support the bridge as it passes over Utah Street, sloping downward to feed into Woodville Road. Designed to carry 20 tons of "live load"(rolling traffic), the bridge was completed in 1931 and opened for traffic on October 28 with great fanfare and blowing of ships' horns. *Submitted by Rick Bryan.*

ALL SAINTS CONGREGATION.
The congregation of All Saints Episcopal Church gathered for this photo with Father Walter Stanley (center), who served as pastor from 1927 to 1940. The church stood at 565 Pinewood Avenue at City Park. Church members gathered for parties and hayrides in the parish hall (at right, facing City Park), heated by a stove at the center of the room. The church was rebuilt at 563 Pinewood in 1948 for $45,000. *Submitted by Berniece Chambers, daughter of Amy Roberts, one of the congregants.*

BIRMINGHAM BEFORE TONY PACKO'S.
This 1930 photograph was taken from an upper window at 1866 Genesee Street, looking north along Genesee toward Consaul Street. At the right is the parish house and the back of St. Stephen's Catholic Church. To the left of the church, just below the Nabisco elevators, are the same buildings on the northwest corner of Consaul and Genesee now being renovated as part of Packo's Hungarian Village development. On the near side of Consaul Street is an old building (now part of a parking lot) that may have been John Packo's restaurant where the young Tony Packo worked before opening his own eatery a couple of years later. *Submitted by Amy Bartus.*

WIRED FOR SECURITY.
This fire and burglary alarm firm began as the Toledo Telegraph and Telephone Messenger Company. By 1930 (when this photo was taken), it was part of the American District Telegraph Company (now ADT). Edward H. Lebowsky (not pictured) managed the Toledo ADT office at 140 Huron Street and later at 140 Michigan Street from 1920 to 1954. His secretary, Jeanette Thomas, married the boss's son, Edward G. Lebowsky. Pictured here (from left): an unidentified gentleman, Alexander Barchick, Earl Clark, another unidentified man, and Roy McFarland. *Submitted by Jeanette (Thomas) Lebowsky and daughter Judy (Lebowsky) Shook.*

UNDER THE HOOD.
Look closely at the second car from the left and you'll see Lieutenant Edward C. Huntington, a clerk with the Toledo Police Bureau of Identification, starting his new Ford Model A four-door the "old-fashioned way" – cranking the motor. The photo was taken March 28, 1931, by fellow officer William H. Stoner from the window of the bureau's offices in the Safety Building. *Submitted by Nancy (Stoner) Stover, granddaughter of 42-year veteran police officer William H. Stoner and daughter of TPD officer William P. Stoner.*

DRIVE RIGHT IN.
Tires, used cars and batteries were for sale at East Side Auto Parts in this late 1930s photo. Still in business at 214 First Street at Oak, the company was started by Charles Kale, a Russian immigrant who came to this country in 1912. He first worked at Willys-Overland until he could afford to buy the old scrap company that became East Side Auto Parts. In the 1930s and 1940s there were many car dealerships nearby on Main Street in East Toledo. The business is still family owned, operated by Charles' son Norty and grandsons Jeff and Andrew Kale. *Submitted by Cindy M. Voller, step-daughter of Norty Kale.*

READ ALL ABOUT IT.
Two members of the Old Newsboys are carrying their papers down Jefferson Avenue circa 1930, ready to distribute them to raise money for charity. The Old Newsboys organization was started by John Gunckel about the turn of the last century to aid the poor children who sold newspapers in the community. When Mr. Gunckel died in 1907, small contributions from hundreds and hundreds of children paid for the large pyramid monument erected at his grave in Woodlawn Cemetery. The tradition of the Old Newsboys – raising money for charity – continues to this day. *Submitted by Tedd Long.*

BUSY BEES.
Norman and his brother Edward Heydinger were both workingmen in 1931. Seen here in the backyard of their Euclid Avenue home, the boys are sporting aprons with the latest slogans for *The Toledo News-Bee* newspaper. Known for its pink color, the *News Bee* was the product of the merger of two papers in 1903, *The Toledo Bee* and the *Toledo News*. The *News-Bee* ceased publication August 2, 1938, citing financial difficulties. *Submitted by Norman Heydinger.*

FAKE OUT.
Francis Lengel, Waite High School running back, is carrying the ball in this rare close-up 1932 photo, probably taken in the old Waite Stadium. He is running toward the camera and appears to have faked the defender before cutting through the hole in the line. Perhaps Toledo's greatest high school back, Lengel played only two years, both championship seasons. After scoring 16 touchdowns his first year, he scored 32 touchdowns and passed for 25 more his second year. That 1932 team scored 382 points and gave up 9. Lengel accounted for 194 of those points: 32 touchdowns and two extra points, in addition to his 25 touchdown passes. In the early part of his career, he didn't even wear a helmet. After leaving Waite, he played basketball for the May Coal Company, semi-pro football with the Jack Frost Sugars, and centerfield with the champion Crimson Coaches fast-pitch softball team. He worked at the Pure Oil Company for 35 years as a water and gas treater. *Submitted by Terrence Lengel, grandson of Francis Lengel.*

WHEN GAS WAS AFFORDABLE.
This classic Sohio service station stood at the corner of Buckingham and Hoag Streets in this 1932 photograph. Although in the depths of the Depression, possibly gasoline was not so affordable even then. The owner was Felix Szymanski, who maintained this little station well, judging by the perfectly manicured hedges. Notice also the tile roof that would have matched the red trim of those early Standard Oil of Ohio stations. *Submitted by Chester R. Szymanski.*

LOOKING FOR ANSWERS.

From his window in the Safety Building, Officer William H. Stoner took this photo in 1931 as a crowd of unemployed citizens converges for answers from Mayor William Jackson. The stock market had crashed on Black Tuesday in 1929, and banks and businesses that had been booming throughout the 1920s were now collapsing, taking jobs with them. Toledo police officers agreed to a ten percent pay cut, city workers were asked to take a week's vacation every month without pay, and the city already owed local grocers half a million dollars for goods provided to families under jobless relief programs. *Submitted by Nancy (Stoner) Stover, granddaughter of William H. Stoner.*

LOOKING TOWARD THE FUTURE.

The 1932 graduating class of St. Mary's Catholic School poses for posterity on the steps of the convent house, next to the school located on Page Street near Jerome. In the front row, third from left, stands a beaming Jeanette Thomas, later Jeanette Lebowsky. It is the last graduation photo for Father William Schiermann, front and center, who was moved to another assignment that year. *Submitted by Judy (Lebowsky) Shook, daughter of Jeanette (Thomas) Lebowsky.*

BATTERIES, TIRES AND BASEBALL.

Young Patty Gaynor (Morse) is on the mound and her cousin Jimmy Erskine is the batter outside their grandpa Chester Erskine's tire and battery shop. The shop was located on the northwest corner of Fearing Boulevard and Wayne Street (now Airport Highway). Looking at the signs, it looks like the shop offered more services than the standard tires and batteries. *Submitted by Cynthia Erskine Rockwell, great-granddaughter of Chester Erskine and daughter of Jimmy Erskine.*

MUSEUM PERISTYLE DEBUT.

Many prominent families in the Toledo area were proud founders and supporters of the Toledo Museum of Art. Turning out in their finest for the opening of the Peristyle in January of 1933 were Marie Pingen Dempsey and dignitaries from around the world. The new Peristyle was funded by Florence Scott and Edward Drummond Libbey. The Philadelphia Orchestra, with legendary conductor Leopold Stokowski, performed for debut night. Part of the concert was broadcast coast-to-coast by CBS. *Submitted by Pamela (Dempsey) Sample, granddaughter of Marie Pingen Dempsey.*

ALL TOGETHER NOW!

Grace Carstensen, 11, plays "The Daring Young Man on the Flying Trapeze" on accordion in 1934 while friends and brother Bobby sing along. Performing in the Campbell driveway at 4351 Willys Parkway at the request of a photographer neighbor, the children are (from left) Patti Kilcourse, Roger Rickenmann, Mary Catherine Kilcourse, Marie Rickenmann, Grace Cartensen, William Campbell, Jack Campbell (who later married Grace), and Bobby Carstensen. *Submitted by Grace Campbell-Potts, who still plays accordion at the holidays.*

CALL IT FATE.
In 1934, Kalman Aharoni (center in white suit), district manager for Schiff Shoes, and the employee by his side, Fannie Miller, 19, were unaware that their lives would be inextricably linked. Fannie left her job soon after this photo and lost contact with her former boss. She married Sam Ravin in 1938 and raised three sons; her first, Beryl, was born in 1939. Thirty years later, at the wedding of a mutual friend, Beryl met and eventually married the woman who captured his heart. At their wedding, Fannie once again stood for a photo beside her former boss. Kalman Aharoni's eldest daughter, Sharon, had just married Beryl Ravin. *Submitted by Sharon (Aharoni) Ravin.*

CATCH OF THE DAY.
Robert V. Oberdorf would one day be a detective in the Toledo Police Department. But in 1936, at the age of 12, he was a *Blade* carrier. In this photograph, taken at 133 Main Street, he proudly displayed his catch of the day. The building behind him is the city's old post office currently home to the VFW. *Submitted by Robin (Oberdorf) Kramer, daughter of Robert Oberdorf.*

FORE FOR FOUR.
A *Toledo Times* reporter joins three city officials posing for a photo during opening day ceremonies for the new Ottawa Park Golf Course on April 5, 1935. Ready to hit the links are, from left, Joseph "Jack" Flanagan, *Toledo Times* political reporter; City Councilman Ira Bame, who served Toledo many years as a municipal judge; Charles J. Mathews, then director of public welfare; and Mayor Solon Klotz, the only socialist to serve as mayor of Toledo. *Submitted by Cindy M. Voller, granddaughter of Judge Ira Bame.*

A LOTTA LETTUCE.
When Sam Okun (far right) started his produce distribution business at 24 N. Huron St., farmers brought their goods to market in horse-drawn wagons. In 1935, when this photo was taken, the company was struggling through the Depression years. Day laborers, called "lumpers," would arrive in the wee hours every morning to unload truckloads of fresh produce so it could be delivered to grocers and restaurants for the day's business. *Submitted by Fred Okun, grandson of Sam Okun.*

WHO THREW THAT?

The splat of snow on the wall between their heads has just put the Njaim brothers on notice that they are targets. George (left) appears to be looking for ammunition to return fire. Maron (right), snowball in hand, seems to be looking at the perpetrator and calculating his throw. The photo was taken in 1936 as the boys were standing outside the Delux grocery market at Norwood and Upton Avenues. The store was owned by their father, Simon Njaim, and the boys helped out there after school. *Submitted by Melissa Callejas, daughter of George Njaim.*

A BOOMING SNACK INDUSTRY.

Kuehmann Potato Chip Company was growing fast in 1936. It was born in the basement of Marie Kuehmann, a German immigrant who began making and selling potato chips in the 1890s to supplement the family income. Her son delivered the chips while her husband ran the grocery upstairs. Mr. Kuehmann died shortly after forming the Kuehmann Potato Chip Company in 1899. Marie and daughter Edythe grew the company for years and sold it to Marie's sons Carl and Rudolph. Rudolph Kuehmann is seen here (center) with other company managers and potato wholesaler Howard J. Nehrig, Sr., second from the left. *Submitted by Ruth Nehrig, wife of Howard J. Nehrig, Jr.*

BUILDING A LEGACY.

The federal Works Progress Administration (WPA) gave many men jobs to feed their families during the years of the Depression, including Stanley Brzezinski. They built a vast number of public facilities, such as the buildings and amphitheater at Walbridge Park, constructed in 1937-38. Here, workers have completed the hillside wall and are creating terraced seating in the hillside. Because of lack of materials, the seating is formed by laying slabs of local rock directly into the hillside. The long-ago site of a family farm and the House of Refuge for orphaned boys, this swath of shoreline later housed an amusement park with a midway and concessions. The city began making moves to buy the land in 1938 at the urging of parks director Thomas Walbridge, entrepreneur and philanthropist, for whom it is named. *Submitted by Chester R. Szymanski, son-in-law of Stanley Brzezinski.*

SEE WHAT'S IN STORE.

Employees at the newest S.S. Kresge Company store – the third in downtown Toledo – sit for a photo in the store's offices. Founded in Detroit, Kresge opened the first Toledo store in 1903 (Summit and Madison) and a second store at 333 Summit Street Store #3 was opened at Adams and St. Clair in 1936. Touted by manager Robert S. Townsend as the first modernistic 5-and-10-cent store of its kind in the world, this new building had air conditioning and was built without interior pillars for an uninterrupted view of the entire retail floor. By 1971, the company had shifted all its attention to its more recent enterprise called Kmart. *Submitted by Joyce Pack.*

MORE THAN TEA.

In 1859, The Great American Tea Company opened its first stores on the east coast. Changing its name to The Great Atlantic and Pacific Tea Company in 1870, the company prospered concentrating on selling more than coffees and teas. The 1920's brought about a new trend – the economy store. Most stores were small and located in the residential areas rather than on the main drag. Cost cutting was key with a staff of one or two, and private label brands such as Eight O'clock coffee, Ann Page and Jane Parker foods. A & P grew leaps and bounds with over sixteen-thousand stores nationwide by the mid 1930s. The store shown here, in 1934, was one of many dotting Toledo neighborhoods. Claude Thomas (left), and Eli Jokinen, behind the register, operated this store at 504 Vance Street. *Submitted by Judy Nickoloff, daughter of Eli Jokinen.*

PLAY BALL!

The town of Booth, Ohio, consisted of two coal yards (Nissen and Gladieux), the Phillips grocery store, Berger's cider mill and a ball diamond where the Booth Red Sox played. Team transportation was the bed of a coal dump truck, courtesy of team manager Marv Nissen. Harry Phillips, the grocer, umpired. In this 1938 photo, the team roster reads (bottom row, from left) Fred Kowalka, William Moritz, batboy Lyle Phillips, Norman Shoemaker, Martin Ruedy (standing) and Dale Phillips, catcher. Second row, from left: Jim Loomis, Mel Phillips, pitcher Roy Moritz, Mel Nelson, Rich Fangman, Howard Berger and Harold Miller. Top row, from left: Marv Nissen, Francis Berger and Norman Joehlin. *Submitted by Roy Moritz.*

THE GATHERING PLACE.
African-Americans in Toledo, whose children were not allowed to attend a "for whites only" neighborhood center, established the Dunbar Center. The Dunbar Center, a place of recreation for African American children, was located on Girard Street. Although activities were limited and equipment, a set of swings, was scarce, the Dunbar Center provided a place for fun during hard times. Rueben Harper, the bell ringer, was the director of the Dunbar Center. Pictured are the children who attended the center in 1939. *Submitted by Lorean Quinn Whitaker.*

A JOB WELL DONE.
These workers at Willys-Overland in the finished car assembly plant look pleased with their work. This picture is from September 1937, and it would not be long before the company would begin gearing up to make the famous World War II general purpose vehicle known as the "Jeep." *Submitted by Chester R. Szymanski.*

GIVING US THE WILLYS.
These Overland workers were photographed in their caps and work clothes on the assembly line in September 1937. They were members of line five, group one. Seated in the second row, second from the right, is John Jiska. Thomas Jiska is behind him at the far right of the third row. Behind Thomas, near the man in the shirt and tie, is Joe Mikloski. *Submitted by Jennifer Wherry.*

DRESSED FOR SUCCESS.
These salesmen and Willys sedans are all lined up at the Koerber Brewery at Oak and Front Streets in East Toledo in 1937. Originally the Home Bottling Company, the brewery was put out of business by prohibition in 1918. Koerber's operated the brewery after 1932 when alcohol was again legalized. Koerber's went out of business in 1950 and the building became a chemical plant, which was destroyed in a tragic explosion in the early 1960s. In this photo, Leonard Sackman stands fifth from the left. *Submitted by Barbara Sackman, daughter of Leonard.*

CAN I STEER?
Ewald Sieler, Jr., poses on the massive rudder of a boat at the shipyards in Toledo. His father was a pattern maker at Toledo Shipbuilding Company on Front Street. The picture was taken when young Ewald was 14 years old in 1938. *Submitted by Joanne Clark, sister of Ewald.*

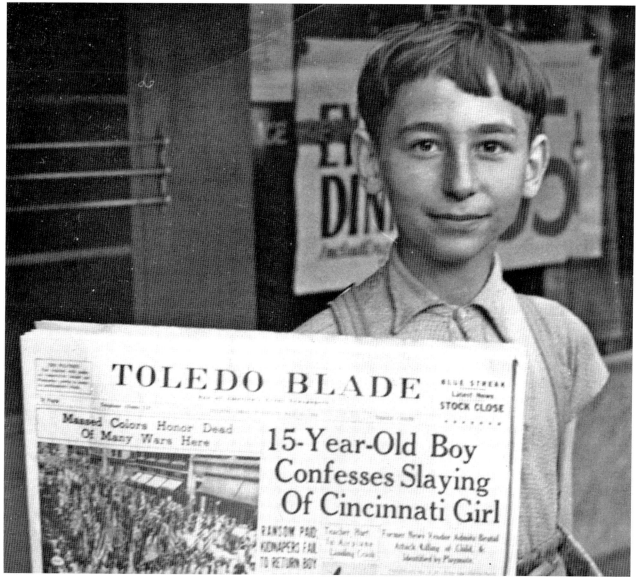

BUY A PAPER, MISTER?

A fresh-faced H. Martin Sitzmann, 11, left Germany with his family in 1937 as tensions rose in pre-WWII Europe. He helped support the family by delivering newspapers and selling the daily *Toledo Blade* in front of the El Pinto Restaurant and the State Theater on Collingwood Boulevard from 1938 to 1942. Dinners at the restaurant behind him cost just 35 cents. The newspaper in his hand sold for 3 cents. *Submitted by H. Martin and Ruth Sitzmann.*

MINDING THE STORE.

Bill Rahe (left, with apron), 14, and Irving "Bud" Moulton, 13, had the complete run of the store on Delence Street at Thurston for a week in 1938. The boys ran the business while Bill's parents took a vacation. A roving photographer stopped in and talked the boys into posing for this shot. Wary of the cost, the boys cooperated anyway, regretting it when the powder in the flash pan went off, creating nearly a foot of rolling smoke along the ceiling and sending the boys into a panic. Once sure there was no fire, they paid the man from the till. *Submitted by Irving "Bud" Moulton.*

THE CANTON AVENUE BOYZ.

Neighborhood friends mug for the camera at one of their favorite spots on Canton Avenue. This snapshot was captured circa 1938 in front of The Silver Moon Café run by Walter Sengail, Sr. The restaurant behind them is the Avenue Café. The lads from the left are Gerald Wright, Richard Saunders, Lionel Ben, Nate Stewart, Clarence Clark, Jesse Covington, Walter Sengail, Jr. and James Stoudamire. *Submitted by the photographer of this photo, Carmen Williamson.*

WORKIN' ON THE RAILROAD.
A crew at the Pier Marquette railroad yard in Erie, Michigan, is shown in this August 1937 picture. In the front row, left to right, are Joe Garcia, Louis Rior, Ralph Hoel and Ed Niswender. In the back row are Joe Curry, John Shinkle, George King and Ed Hoel. It is assumed the railroad ran more than the handcar shown in this photo. *Submitted by Evelyn (Oswald) Buchholtz.*

FOR THE BOYS.
Marian "Mina" Dana entertained the troops in France during World War I as a concert pianist and accompanist, sponsored by the YMCA. After the war, living on Oak Grove Place, she wore the uniform of the Women's Overseas Service League, founded in 1921 by women who had served in World War I. WOSL was the first women's organization to contribute to UNICEF and one of the first to be an accredited observer at the United Nations. Ms. Dana's career took her to Chicago, but she retired in Toledo to be near her sister, Grace Stahl, wife of Common Pleas Judge Scott Stahl, and married for the first time at age 69. *Submitted by Grace Campbell-Potts, grandniece of Marian Dana.*

ABOUT TOWN.
In decades past, shopping was more than "running errands." It was a festive outing that required your Sunday best: a hat, a dress, and an occasional pair of white gloves. A determined Mrs. Avery, an unknown shopper-in-training and Shirley Beebe (Maxfield) are dressed for a successful trip downtown circa 1940. *Submitted by Shirley Maxfield.*

CINDERELLA CARROLL.
Owens-Illinois "Cinderella" winner Ruth Carroll (Rankin) holds the end of a glass-blowing tube for a publicity photo in 1940. "Cinderella Carroll" represented Toledo at the World's Fair in New York City that same year. *Submitted by David Rankin.*

THE ICEMAN COMETH.
Jim Taylor and his grandpa, Harry Coe, wait patiently on the porch of their 1935 Ontario Street home for the ice man. On delivery day, customers would hang the preprinted sign on the front of the house with the number of pounds of ice needed at the twelve o'clock position. The ice was delivered by horse drawn wagon. On this day in 1941 Jim's folks only needed 25 pounds of ice. *Submitted by Jim Taylor.*

MEMORIES ON FILM.
Andrew Aranyosi purchased this building in 1939, making his home in the back of it. The storefront he leased to his brother Joe, a photographer. Joe opened Aranyosi's Studio here at 220 Paine Avenue. For more than 20 years, from this tiny shop, Mr. Aranyosi photographed families and special occasions to preserve memories for the generations to come. *Submitted by Andrew Aranyosi, son of Andrew, Sr.*

SWEETS FOR THE SWEET.

This little candy store stood next to the Valentine Theater at 405 N. St. Clair Street at Adams in the 1940s and early 1950s. It was called M & R Lunch, for owners Norman "Bob" Reed and Morley Michael, who also owned other similar shops. (Notice the big orange behind the counter through the open doorway). *Submitted by Mary Fischer, Ruth Nehrig and Helen Schramm, daughters of Norman "Bob" Reed.*

DRINK TO YOUR HEALTH.

The M & R Diner and "Soda Grille" at 237 Summit Street featured their orange health drink that was "good and good for you." Like their candy store next to the Valentine Theater on St. Clair Street, this charming 1950s Art Deco diner offered fruit drinks to early health-conscious customers. They also offered to non-weight watchers an M & R malted milk or a rich chocolate soda for 15 cents. *Submitted by Mary Fischer, Ruth Nehrig and Helen Schramm, daughters of co-owner Norman "Bob" Reed.*

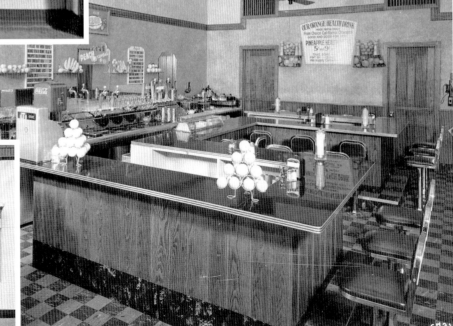

DELUXE DELIVERY.
Dry cleaning has firm roots at 1233 Sylvania Avenue. Edward Pollex built the DeLuxe Cleaners building in 1933. The shop's success can be seen in its fleet of delivery trucks out front. Customers trusted DeLuxe Cleaners with everything from feathered hats and fine furs to furniture, due to the careful work of people like Walter Beham, who worked here for 50 years. He still worked here in 1978, when William Nunemaker bought the business and changed its name to the current Lincoln Cleaners. *Submitted by Mary K. (Mrs. Walter) Beham.*

IT'S A WRAP!

Chase Bag Company, founded in 1847, established a plant in Toledo in 1925 at Brown and Nebraska Avenues. Here, in 1940, Charles Davis stands behind the large rolls of paper awaiting transformation into paper sacks. The parent company celebrated its 100th anniversary in 1947 with an open house for employees, families and guests. It was still operating locally as late as the 1990s. *Submitted by Naomi Davis, wife of Charles Davis.*

PLACE YOUR ORDER.

Tiedtke's Department Store was the nation's first supermarket – the first store of its kind where shoppers could buy all their groceries in one place. Tiedtke's was especially known for its cheese and produce departments. Aromas from the bakery tempted shoppers from other areas of the store. In this photo from 1940, produce clerk Wilbur Smeltzer, right, poses with a co-worker. *Submitted by Ruth Smeltzer.*

CHARITY BEGINS AT HOME.

During World War II, Frank Baker (of the B.R. Baker Shoe Company) and his family opened their home to many young sailors stationed at the Naval Training School at Bay View Park for 13 weeks of training before going off to war. Baker's family and coworkers would meet the naval trainees at the base and invite them to their homes. The Bakers brought them to their riverside cabin (they called the "Mud Shack") for home-cooked turkey dinners, kegs of beer and family hospitality. Here, Amelia Baker plays piano while sister Bernice (standing) leads the vocals. *Submitted by Bernice (Baker) Langenderfer.*

WAITING FOR THE TRAIN.

The Baker family had a small cabin just a mile upriver from Vollmar Park on Route 65. Bernice Baker, standing behind a gondola car, waits to ride the train while the engineer places coal in the engine car during a trip there in 1941. Bernice and friends frequently came to the park by boat to ride the train and round or square dance in the dance hall above the beer garden. Vollmar Park was a family tradition; her mother's family was among the many that traveled there from Toledo by horse and buggy – an all-day trip that required an overnight stay in the hotel at the parks entrance. *Submitted by Bernice (Baker) Langenderfer.*

A GEM OF A STORE.
The Osterman & Levey jewelry store near the corner of Summit and Adams Streets was a fixture in downtown Toledo in the 1940s. The original store opened its doors in 1928 in the Toledo Trust Building on Superior near Madison Avenue. *Submitted by Bob Levey, son of Ruby Levey, co-owner of the jewelry store.*

OSTERMAN AND LEVEY.
Ruby Levey and Lewis N. Osterman, Sr., celebrate the 19th anniversary of Osterman & Levey Jewelers in 1947. Ruby Levey died on May 19, 1959. The Levey name was dropped from the store's title in 1965. *Submitted by Bob Levey, son of Ruby Levey.*

ADVANCE GLOVE WAS ADVANCED.
Once called the "glove center of the Midwest," Toledo was also considered the center of the glove industry for a large part of the entire country. Advance Glove Company was located at 122 Southard Street downtown. Originally headquartered in Detroit in 1934, it moved to Toledo in 1939 and eventually served industrial users in many parts of Europe and South America. Most of the major manufacturing firms in Toledo bought from Advance Glove. In 1959, the company was turning out an average of 28,000 pairs of gloves a day in some 500 different types including canvas, terry cloth and goatskin. Machine operators like the women seen in this 1940s photo were considered specialists – some sewed on the thumbs, others the fingers, and still others, the cuffs. *Submitted by Corrine Gauthier.*

NO UGLY DUCKLING.
More peaceful than the Whip, the Swan was another amusement ride in Walbridge Park in the 1940s. Betty Manning and daughters Barbara, Mary Jane and even little Donna Jean could relax and enjoy the view of the parking lot as the giant swan circles around the shallow pool. This photo was taken about 1946 or 1947. *Submitted by Delphine Purnia, sister of Betty Manning.*

WELCOME TO OUR HOME.
Delia and Thomas Marlowe pose here at their home at 2729 Collingwood Boulevard in the 1940s. Mr. Marlowe, who died in 1965 at the age of 96, came from County Cork, Ireland. He arrived in Toledo in 1899, and in 1906 helped found the Citizen's Ice Company, where he remained until his retirement in 1949. A massive Citizen's Ice building still stands on Nevada Street near East Broadway in East Toledo. *Submitted by Carol Arnold and Nancy Ligibel.*

A MEAL FOR A NICKEL.
Hamburgers were inexpensive at Triangle Lunch in the 1940s. The first Triangle Lunch, seen here, opened in April of 1935 on Monroe Street at Detroit Avenue, directly across the street from Toledo's historic Swayne Field. (Note the sign at right, warning sports fans to park elsewhere.) That year, The University of Toledo Rockets played their first night football game at Swayne Field (a 20-0 victory over the Capital team). Swayne Field was built on land donated by Noah H. Swayne, an avid baseball fan and son of U.S. Supreme Court Justice (1862-1881) Noah H. Swayne. A devout Quaker, Swayne was appointed to the court by President Abraham Lincoln for his anti-slavery stance. (Mr. Swayne is profiled in the first edition of *Toledo: Our Life, Our Times, Our Town*). *Submitted by Perry Zeigler.*

SUPER MARKET.
Before supermarkets became widespread, every neighborhood had a corner market, often the friendliest and safest place to "hang out" close to home. Van's Market at 1111 Michigan Street was that kind of place in 1945. Here, owner William Van Hall poses in front of his store with Sherrie Dorah (left) and Denny Saba. *Submitted by Sally Saba, stepdaughter of William Van Hall.*

COBBLER IN THE WINDOW.

A craftsman demonstrates how he makes his employer's brand of hand-made shoes, one of many innovative publicity ideas developed by Frank Baker. Hired as a boy by his uncle, founder B.R. Baker, Frank Baker rose to vice president of Toledo's B.R. Baker Clothing Company before retiring. The store's "invisible" windows were non-reflective for far better viewing, an attraction that inspired creative and unusual displays. The cobbler in the window, Benjamin Boody, was brought in for a week in 1940 to demonstrate the value of comfortable, well-made men's shoes, courtesy of the shoe manufacturer. The price for a pair of these hand-made shoes: 12 dollars.

Submitted by Dolores (Baker) Eberly, daughter of Frank Baker and 10-year B.R. Baker employee.

DRESSED TO IMPRESS.
These fine young men are posing in front of the Third Baptist Church (established in 1868) at 402 Pinewood Avenue in the 1940s. The gentlemen in front (from left) are Virgil Chauncy (now a retired postal clerk), Aubry Bufkin (now a retired postal carrier) and Jerome Nealy; those standing behind (from left) are Hamilton Allen (former Ohio Lottery director in Toledo, retired), Richard McCown (now a retired accountant) and Navarro Gibson (who graduated from the University of Mexico, Mexico City, and taught Spanish and art in Chicago and Toledo schools). *Submitted by Equilla (Gibson) Roach, sister of Navarro Gibson.*

AND THEY MEANT ANYWHERE.
On Christmas Eve, 1941, Morris Hirsch moved his newsstand indoors at this 319 St. Clair Street address. At this store and the Adams Street location after 1959, Hirsch's Bookstore kept many Toledoans well-read and carried daily newspapers from 200 cities. With his wife, Fay (whom he called "Miss Smith" at the store), he did a booming business shipping books to servicemen during World War II. Jack Dempsey and Al Kaline signed books here; Mr. Hirsch was a fan of baseball and boxing. *Photo submitted by Gordon Hirsch, son of Morris Hirsch.*

FULL SERVICE.
The Wagar Brothers gas station did a brisk business in automotive fuel, tires and repair services at the corner of Upton and Georgia Avenues from 1927 to 1958. This is a typical busy day in the 1940s for Sherman "Shorty" Wagar, first on the left, and his brother Edmund, fourth from the right. *Submitted by Mrs. Jack Wagar, daughter-in-law of Edmund.*

AT THE PHARMACY.
Customers and employees gather around the lunch counter in the Paul Losser Pharmacy at Lawrence Avenue and Monroe Street, December 1949. Seen here, from left, are pharmacist "Bob," tobacconist Dick Miller, two customers, a member of the pharmacy wait staff, a customer, and Ruth Smeltzer and Lillian Miller. *Submitted by Ruth Smeltzer.*

WHAT A BARGAIN!
Based on the prices posted behind Helen and Ed Rucki, you could purchase a bag full of groceries for less than five dollars in the late 1940s. Rucki's Market opened for business in 1947 at South Erie and Hobart Streets in South Toledo. *Submitted by Helene Sheets, granddaughter of Helen and Ed Rucki.*

LEFT. LEFT. LEFT, RIGHT, LEFT.
Members of the State Guard, 37th Division, are marching down Jefferson Avenue past the Lamson Department Store on the right. Future Toledo mayor and Ohio governor Michael V. DiSalle was a lieutenant in one of the two Toledo Guard units. It was probably Memorial Day, as indicated by the decorations and all the children at the right holding flags. *Submitted by Paul Rehfeldt.*

SWINGIN' HIGH.
Swingin' Toledo has always been a great town for music, from jazz to blues to rock and everything in between. In the 1940s, swing bands were all the rage. The Gibson Band pictured here included, from left, Carl Anderson, Charles Gibson, Tommy Alexander and Larry Rodgers. *Submitted by Joyce (Gibson) Brown and Equilla (Gibson) Roach, daughters of Charles Gibson.*

NICE DAY FOR A SALE.
Sam Manera drove his sister Virginia (Miracola) downtown to hunt for bargains one spring morning in 1940. A Tiedtke's banner hanging in the background suggests that is where the future bride was headed for a last-minute item or two. *Submitted by Ginny and Don Smith, daughter and son-in-law of Virginia.*

READY FOR TAKEOFF.
Toledo Municipal Airport has changed since Richard Layman was photographed on his motorcycle circa 1940. Taken when Mr. Layman was about 18, the picture shows interesting details of an early motorbike. Even though he wasn't wearing a helmet, Mr. Layman has survived to the age of 83 and lives in Rudolph, Ohio. *Submitted by Joan Rumpf.*

SINGING HIS PRAISES.
Third Baptist Church is one of the oldest churches in Toledo, founded in 1868. This photo of the Melody C Choir in 1940 was taken in the chapel at 402 Pinewood. The choir members are (front row, from left) Druscilla Gibson, Mary Oates, Equilla Gibson, Ruth Johnson, Roberta Smith, Jesse Oates, Joyce Gibson and choir leader Mrs. Clara Farrell. Back row, from left: the Rev. Calvin Stallmaker, Charles Gibson, Jr., Octavia Davis, Jean Lear, Louise Lawson, Doris Lawson, Ernestine Smith, Rosetta Smith and Catherine Johnson. *Submitted by Joyce (Gibson) Brown, sister to Charles Gibson, Jr., Druscilla Gibson and Equilla (Gibson) Roach.*

PROUD PUPPETEERS.
Dressed in their Brownie uniforms, Carolyn Anderson (far left), Mary Ann Lindsay (center) and Marilyn Otto proudly display their hand-made rag doll marionettes. The girls made the puppets in 1945 as a project of Brownie Troop 92 at Collingwood Methodist Episcopal Church. *Submitted by Beverly Miner and the archives of the Girl Scout Council of Maumee Valley.*

A VIEW FROM THE TOP.
Downtown Toledo was a hub of business and entertainment for many years. This 1940s glimpse of the hustle and bustle was captured by Norman Witherell looking north on St. Clair Street from top of the Ohio Building, where he worked. *Submitted by Ron Westphal, grandson of Norman.*

STEP RIGHT UP!
In these photos from the 1940s, visitors to the Ringling Bros. Barnum & Bailey Circus are walking past sideshow banners while the circus is being set up with the help of elephants. The large field on Manhattan Boulevard, where the circus was held, is presently the site of a Kmart store. These banners, incidentally, have increased in value as works of art, and today can fetch more than $10,000. *Submitted by Robert Schaefer.*

JEEPS FOR THE GIs.

In 1943, women supported the war effort in many ways, including as employees of the Cleveland Ordnance District, responsible for the procurement and distribution of ordnance and equipment, equipment maintenance and repair and development and testing of new types of ordnance. That included Jeeps and parts made in Toledo. Pictured in these Jeeps at the Toledo Willys-Overland plant are: (front row, from left) Alice Zenk (passenger), Grace Carstensen (at the wheel in the second Jeep) and Nadalyn Abelowitz and Libby Kambas (third Jeep). Second row, fourth Jeep from left, at the wheel is Hazel Mohn. *Submitted by Stuart Campbell, son of Grace (Carstensen) Campbell-Potts.*

BACK IN SERVICE.

In the early 1940s, Marian "Mina" Dana held a luncheon in her home at 2405 Oak Grove Place for local members of the Women's Overseas Service League. No doubt the women had already re-launched programs of support for U.S. troops now fighting a new war in Europe. Mina is seated in the front row, far right. *Submitted by Grace Campbell-Potts.*

STRIKE UP THE BAND.
Poised and ready to blow, James Huber (on trumpet second from the right) and his band, the Royal Venetians, are assembled on the bandstand at the Trianon Ballroom in the early 1940s. James' love for music kept him playing from the late 1920s to 1976. Big names such as Artie Shaw and Duke Ellington, also played at the Trianon. *Submitted by Terry Huber, son of James.*

FISKE BROTHERS FIRE.
Many people came to watch the huge clouds of smoke billowing from the Fiske Brothers Refinery on Oakdale Avenue on September 27, 1942. The East Side refinery made highly flammable lubricant products. Fiske Brothers rebuilt and is still in business at the same location more than 60 years after this spectacular fire. *Submitted by Charlotte Carr Hendrickson.*

SOME R & R.

A summer drive in 1947 ends with a detour to Side Cut Park where John Calmes and Lourine Pollauf enjoy a little rest and relaxation. Side Cut received its name from the side cut extension of the Erie and Miami Canal that once connected the main line with Maumee. It was the first metropark, established in 1930. Three of the six original locks from the canal system can still be seen in the area's metroparks. *Submitted by daughter Connie Calmes.*

BUY WAR BONDS.

Many celebrities pitched in to help the war effort in the 1940s. Among them was Marlene Dietrich, seen here at a Toledo rally in 1942. Ms. Dietrich left Germany in the 1930s and became a U.S. citizen in 1937. She was in Toledo for two days as part of a Jeep Caravan tour to promote sales of war bonds in Ohio. Seated next to her is then Mayor John Q. Carey, who headed the local organization of aid for the Allied defense, which included raising money through war bonds. Months later, Mayor Carey resigned the office after he was elected to fill an unexpired term on the Common Pleas Court. *Submitted by Anne O'Shea.*

HOME ON LEAVE.
Carl Kutz embraces family members at home on Centennial Road in 1942 before heading off to war in the Philippines. Family members are, from left, sisters Gertrude and Clara, Carl, mother Hulda, brother Norman, and an unidentified relative. In front, brother William hugs sister Florence. Carl earned two Purple Hearts and contracted malaria before returning home in 1945. He married Gladys Turnow and had two sons before the malaria that lay dormant flared up and became fatal. *Submitted by Fred Kutz, who lost his father, Carl, at age 13.*

TAKING A MINUTE.
A dapper Charlie Hong was spotted relaxing outside the Kin Wa Low restaurant/cabaret on Cherry Street. The restaurant was owned by Ha Sun Loo, Charlie's father-in-law. With three floor shows scheduled for this 1942 night, it's a wonder Charlie had the time for this snapshot. *Submitted by Howard Loo, son of Ha Su Loo and brother-in-law of Charlie.*

"V" IS FOR VICTORY.
The streets of downtown Toledo were jam-packed with everyone trying to get a good spot along the Victory Parade route in July of 1942. The folks perched in the windows of the Spitzer Building have the best view as men and women from all branches of service march up Madison Avenue. *Submitted by Howard Loo.*

A GREAT DAY FOR SAILING.
This February 1942 photograph shows the Holman family preparing for some ice boating on Maumee Bay. Mel and his mother, Ursula, are seen here, while in the background father Melvin puts the finishing touches on the boat he built, *Arctic II*. *Submitted by Judy and Mel Holman.*

A RIVER RUNS AROUND IT.

Before Libbey High School was built, the city had to make room by changing the course of Swan Creek. Edward Drummond Libbey donated $35,000 for the task. (The creek runs just behind the school.) Libbey opened in 1923 with 1500 students. Its football stadium was built with funds from Florence Scott Libbey in 1927. In 1941, not only were the Libbey Cowboys airborne (when this was taken for the yearbook), they also had Libbey's best football record to date and went on to the state football championship, where the game was called a deadlock, 14-14. *Submitted by Naomi Davis, 1941 Libbey graduate and former secretary for the LHS Industrial Arts Department.*

PROMISING FUTURE.
Ready for any medical emergency, this group of young ladies is all smiles after completing the 1943 Toledo Hospital School of Nursing program. THSN's predecessor, the Toledo Training School, graduated its first class of five students in 1895 from their Cherry and Sherman Streets location. Toledo Hospital moved to its North Cove Boulevard home in December of 1929. The Croxton House for Nurses on Oatis Avenue opened in January of 1930 to house nursing students. The THSN graduated its last class in June of 1988. *Submitted by Corrine Gauthier.*

GONE TO GOON'S.
Leo Bass (pictured) lived with his sister Cecelia's family, the Slowinskis, and bought his cigars at Goon's Drugs at 1943 Dorr Street. Families came there for its soda fountain and especially for its ice cream. Its owner, Warren Goon, was a druggist and ice cream manufacturer. Goon Ice Cream started at 2101 Dorr Street and became one of the area's largest ice cream plants before he sold the business to Borden's in 1946. In the '70s, another druggist bought the store, making new owner and pharmacist Thomas J. Hutton the only black owner of a full-service drug store in Toledo. *Submitted by Dolores (Lendecker) Slowinski, daughter-in-law of Cecelia (Bass) and Bob Slowinski.*

THE CORNER STORE.
Until the late 1950s, families shopped at corner grocery stores like Knudel's, at 2121 Dorr St. near Parkside Boulevard. Most were family businesses; children in this neighborhood "hung out" here and called the owners Grandma and Grandpa Knudel. Mary Ann Slowinski was one of seven children in a family that couldn't easily afford the handmade chocolates sold here. But the children came running when the Silvercup Bakery deliveryman arrived. He gave the children treasures: free miniature loaves of bread. *Submitted by Stephen and Mary Ann (Slowinski) Binkowski.*

CHRISTMAS AT GRANDMA'S.
Mom and Dad Taylor set sons Jim (left), age 5, and Denny, 2, in front of the family Christmas tree for photos at their grandparents' (Catherine and Harry Coe) home on Ontario Street in 1943. In the very next photo, the two boys' expressions were quite different after having been scolded for acting up. Their uncle Robert Coe and his friends in the 9th Armored Division got quite a kick out of them. They were training on the West Coast before shipping out to the North African front. Robert Coe was captured during the Battle of the Bulge and held as a prisoner of war. *Submitted by Denny Taylor.*

PHOSPHATE WHILE YOU WAIT?
Like many drugstores in the 1940s, the Meyer Drug Co. on Broadway at South Avenue sold dry goods and soda fountain treats as well as pharmacy goods. Here, in 1944, pharmacist/owner Earl W. Meyer shows a thing or two to son Robert, while Earl, Jr. looks on (far right). The boys and their sister, Patricia (now Patricia Wheeler), worked part-time at the store, often impressing dates with after-hours access to the soda fountain while dad locked up. *Submitted by Robert Meyer, son of Earl Meyer, Sr.*

TEE-TOTALER AND TAVERN.
Leonard Sackman spent his entire working life with beer and whiskey, but he never drank a drop. The son of a brewery salesman, Leonard "inherited" his father's territory then moved on to a second brewery. After managing Bob's Grill, located in the building behind the Commodore Perry Hotel, Leonard and Bill Kuenzel opened the B&L Bar at Michigan and Magnolia Streets. They did a good business with the "shot and a beer" crowd (note all the bottles of Calvert whiskey up front), serving lunch and cashing checks for the many employees from the Autolite plant two blocks away. He owned the bar until the early 1970s. *Submitted by Barbara Sackman, daughter-in-law of Leonard Sackman.*

BIG MAC.

The 1944 photo, left, shows a crowd gathered to watch the *Mackinaw* lowered into the water during construction at the American Shipbuilding Company on Front Street. The U. S. Coast Guard Cutter *Mackinaw* was a 290-foot vessel specifically designed for ice breaking on the Great Lakes, built at a cost of 10 million dollars beginning in 1942. Her first commanding officer, Edwin J. Roland, later served as Commandant of the Coast Guard. The grand vessel, known as "Big Mac," was a familiar sight on the lakes for over 60 years. Due to age and expensive upkeep, the *Mackinaw* was decommissioned on June 10, 2006, and replaced by a smaller cutter also called the *Mackinaw*. The old *Mackinaw* moved under her own power to a permanent dock at her namesake port, Mackinaw City, Michigan. *Submitted by Julius Nagy.*

YOU CAN BE SURE OF SHELL.
A stack of tires by the garage door and three pumps – none of which took credit cards: this was the Shell station at the corner of Woodville Road and Navarre Avenue, pictured here in 1944. Emmert Blasingame was the owner. His grandchildren still remember playing in his Hudson Terraplane, a car that was popular in the 1930s, and still is among automobile enthusiasts. *Submitted by Tom Hillabrand.*

HANG ON TIGHT!
The Whip was a popular ride when Walbridge was an amusement park. In this photo, Betty Manning and two of her daughters, Barbara and Mary Jane, are enjoying the excitement. This picture was taken shortly before the Whip was dismantled about 1947. *Submitted by Delphine Purnia, sister of Betty Manning.*

TEST DRIVE.
Madeline Larberg (Drozdowicz) and friend take a break from test-driving Jeeps for Willys-Overland Motors in 1944. They pose at the intersection of Lewis and Phillips Avenues, wearing company-furnished uniforms: aviator helmets, fur-lined gloves, wool slacks and parkas. *Submitted by Madeline Drozdowicz.*

ON MY HONOR...

When the Toledo Area Boy Scout Council bought the land in 1917, it was a long way from the city of Toledo. Camp Miakonda opened for camping in 1924. Since then, boy scouts have come to this woodland camp for up to two weeks to experience the outdoors, learn canoeing and other skills, and build character. These scouts attended the camp in 1944. During World War II, when many young fathers were serving overseas, scouting programs like these became even more important to Toledo's young boys. *Submitted by Joseph P. Hanley, II (second scout from the right).*

SORTING SPUDS.

Workers process potatoes at the produce operation owned by Howard J. Nehrig, Sr. at 31-35 Huron in 1944. The handsome fellow keeping an eye on the potatoes as they fall through the chute into bags (second from the right) is the owner's son, Howard Nehrig, Jr. One of several produce distributors in downtown Toledo, H. J. Nehrig supplied the Kuehmann Potato Chip factory, one of six in town. *Submitted by Ruth Nehrig, wife of Howard J. Nehrig, Jr.*

PICNIC IN THE PARK.
For decades, Riverside Park has been the site of innumerable events. In 1944, Joan Webber (center, holding cake) had just graduated from high school. She was at the park with the Long family enjoying time with their son Ray (center, just left of Joan in background), who was home on leave from the U.S. Navy. *Submitted by Joan Rumpf.*

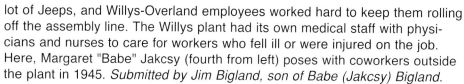

HELP ON THE LINE.
World War II demanded a lot of Jeeps, and Willys-Overland employees worked hard to keep them rolling off the assembly line. The Willys plant had its own medical staff with physicians and nurses to care for workers who fell ill or were injured on the job. Here, Margaret "Babe" Jakcsy (fourth from left) poses with coworkers outside the plant in 1945. *Submitted by Jim Bigland, son of Babe (Jakcsy) Bigland.*

OH, CHRISTMAS TREE.
The war was still going on in Europe at Christmastime in 1944, and people back home needed something to celebrate. These soon-to-be Christmas trees being unloaded by Howard Nehrig, Jr. (left) and brother William Horace Nehrig must have been a welcome sight. Howard has stopped to show a tree to the secretary for his father's wholesale produce company, H.J. Nehrig. *Submitted by Ruth Nehrig, wife of Howard J. Nehrig, Jr.*

DOWNTOWN PARADE. A Chamber of Commerce float maneuvers around the corner in front of Toledo's old post office in the Toledo Trust Building at St. Clair and Madison. Dale Beaudry is at the wheel. It is believed that this parade was thrown to honor Sgt. Alex Drabik, WWII hero. Note the two women poised on the ledge four stories above the 1945 parade route. *Submitted by Dale Beaudry.*

VICTORY BOND DRIVE.
Nancy Bella and Mary Frech are sitting in Adolph Hitler's personal Mercedes Benz as part of a war bond effort in Toledo in 1945. It appears the car was being displayed in the lobby of Toledo Trust at Madison Avenue and Superior Street, attracting many onlookers and potential bond purchasers. *Submitted by Nancy (Bella) Brown Schott.*

BREAKFAST OF CHAMPIONS.
Major League Baseball outfielder and first baseman Roy Cullenbine autographs boxes of Wheaties cereal for his fans at Tiedtke's circa 1945. Mr. Cullenbine, a Mud Hens outfielder in 1937, also played for the Brooklyn Dodgers, St. Louis Browns, Washington Senators, NY Yankees and Cleveland Indians. He was part of the Detroit Tigers, 1945 World Series Championship team and led the American League in walks that same year, with 113. *Submitted by Shirley Ignasiak.*

CELEBRATING VICTORY.

The Chinese Relief Association of Toledo was developed to aid Chinese immigrants. The group helped recent immigrants get established and assisted those already here in bringing their families to the United States. This photo, taken in the present Toledo Spain Plaza, showed the group in September, 1945, after a Victory Day Parade. Seated in the second row, far left, is Wing Fong, co-owner of the Kin Wa Low restaurant and nightclub. Fifth from the right, in the same row, is his son, Hing Fong, who worked there as a cook, and in the third row, standing, sixth from left, is his cousin, Rank Chin Loo. *Submitted by John Loo.*

FOUR GAL FRIDAYS?

Four students pose for this photo outside Harriet Whitney High School in May of 1946: (from left) Marcianne Korpik, Rosa Sieja, Dorothy Tagsold and Joan Hildebrand. Whitney was built in 1939 as a vocational school for girls, where young women would prepare for jobs then open to them and learn to operate those newfangled business machines (mimeographs, etc.). Named for a woman who taught in one of Toledo's first one-room schoolhouses a century earlier, Whitney opened a year after Macomber Vocational School for boys, directly across the street (the building in the background). *Submitted by Stephen and Mary Ann (Slowinski) Binkowski.*

IT BEGAN WITH DIAPERS.

The founders of the Tiny Tot Diaper Service in 1946, Alvin and Edna Shnider, knew that luck had a lot to do with the success of any business. Mr. Shnider apparently had a lot of luck. After selling Tiny Tot, he proceeded to start 27 more businesses in the 45 years between leaving the service after World War II and 1990. The list includes many household names for Toledoans: two Putt-Putt locations, the Zip'z Ice Cream at Douglas and Monroe, and a significant investment in the chain of Ontario discount stores. He also was a founder of Sunshine Children's Home, served on the Toledo Zoning Board and Port Authority advisory board, and was very active in United Appeals and Community Chest (now combined within the United Way), the Old Newsboys Scholarship Fund and the Volunteers of America. *Submitted by Ron Shnider, son of Alvin and Edna Shnider.*

MAKE A WISH.

Ha Sun Loo celebrates his 50th birthday in 1946 with friends, family and patrons at his entertainment phenomenon, the Kin Wa Low. Seated left to right behind the railing: Judge Harvey Straub, Ha Sun Loo, wife Lee Shee Loo, son-in-law Charlie Hong and daughter Betty Hong. Located at 613 Cherry St., the restaurant expanded over time to encompass five storefronts and was a shining jewel in Toledo's nightlife. Ha Sun owned and operated the Chinese-American theater/restaurant until his health required him to have son-in-law Charlie Hong and daughter Betty take over daily operations. His son Howard later joined the management team.

Known for its hydraulic dance floor and ornate interior, Kin Wa Low was the hot spot for special occasions from proms and office parties to anniversaries. International superstars Ella Fitzgerald and Bobby Darin graced the stage, but the biggest week ever belonged to Toledo's own Helen O'Connell. The era ended when Howard Loo could no longer afford the costs to fight the IRS over a cabaret tax. The restaurant was seized in lieu of the debt in 1958. The building was razed in 1965 for senior citizen housing. *Submitted by Myrna and Howard Loo, daughter-in-law and son of Ha Sun Loo.*

HAVE CLEAVER, WILL TRAVEL.
With his pint-sized apron and grown up meat cutting tools, two-year-old Richard Maxfield means business. Richard and family lived behind the Midway Market at 2837 Albion Street. The market was operated by his mom's cousin, Etta Crandall. *Submitted by Shirley Maxfield, mother of Richard.*

MAKING A SPLASH IN TOLEDO.
Jean Cook and Virginia Spoon pose for a picture in front of the fountain at the Civic Center Mall on Jackson Street in 1947. *Submitted by Linda Wing, daughter of Jean (Cook) Wilkinson.*

SUNNY DAYS RETURN.
In the post-war years of the 1940s, the economy was booming and life was good, especially at Cedar Point Beach. Finally, men and women could put the misery and losses of war behind them and return with confidence to the joys of youthful flirting. After a day of swimming and lounging on the sand with friends, many headed to Cedar Point to dance the night away in the Grand Ballroom to music played by the best big bands in the nation. *Submitted by Ted Prisby.*

CREATING A MASTERPIECE.
Louis Heilbrun, a baker for Tiedtke's Department Store, puts the finishing touches on this cake created for the celebration of the 50th anniversary of the Fred Christen & Sons Co., roofing contractors in this photo taken in 1947. The actual building, then known as the Central Labor Union Building, is still standing on Adams and 10th Streets, across from the Main Library. Mr. Heilbrun worked for Tiedtke's more than 25 years. *Submitted by Louis Heilbrun.*

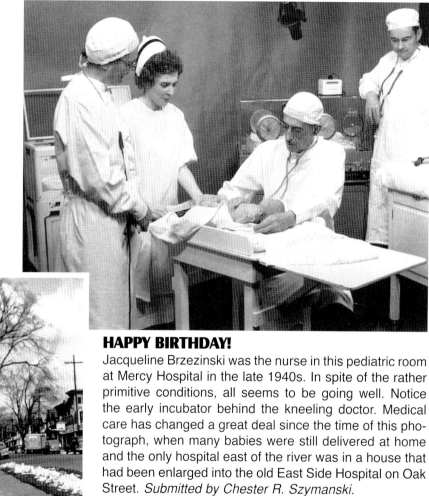

HAPPY BIRTHDAY!
Jacqueline Brzezinski was the nurse in this pediatric room at Mercy Hospital in the late 1940s. In spite of the rather primitive conditions, all seems to be going well. Notice the early incubator behind the kneeling doctor. Medical care has changed a great deal since the time of this photograph, when many babies were still delivered at home and the only hospital east of the river was in a house that had been enlarged into the old East Side Hospital on Oak Street. *Submitted by Chester R. Szymanski.*

WHO'S WALKING WHOM?
In March 1949, Charles Brown is bundled up and ready to embark on an adventure with his dog, Teddy. Before they venture out on East Woodruff Avenue near Vermont Street, they pose for the camera. *Submitted by Donald Brown.*

AND A HAPPY NEW YEAR.
Ladies at the 1950 Libbey-Owens-Ford Christmas party gather to lead the caroling. The company had plenty to sing about in 1947 and things were only getting better. LOF set new records for sales, production, net earnings, jobs and payroll in 1948. By 1950, they would be expanding at two plants, patenting new automotive glass formulas and forming methods, introducing nonconductive glass for commercial electronics applications (it was kept secret for the military during the war), and providing another product to encase and protect the nation's most prized documents: the original Declaration of Independence and U.S. Constitution. The singers are (from left) Winnie (Kennedy) Eisenhower (first wife of local bootlegger and Licavoli gang hit target Jack Kennedy), Lorna Bowerschmidt, Polly Jay, Jean Kuhlman, Helen Rowe, Kay Schurman, Refa Defon and Princess Harrison. *Submitted by Jeanny Amidon and Rick Bryan.*

ROOT, ROOT, ROOT FOR THE HOME TEAM.
Once upon a time in America, companies treated their employees like members of the family. The Krantz Brewing Company on Lagrange Street near Oakland made Old Dutch Beer – and sponsored a baseball team. To help them kick off the season – or perhaps to celebrate a victory – the company held a parade down Lagrange Street for its team. Note that the company had its own marching band, and that the baseball players marched last. *Submitted by Ted Grachek.*

IT BEGAN WITH MARIE.

In 1899, having demonstrated to her husband, Charles, that her homemade potato chips were undeniably more financially successful than his grocery store, Marie Kuehmann started the Kuehmann Potato Chip Company. Charles died soon thereafter, and Marie pushed on, opening a factory at 1105 Dorr Street in 1910. By 1947, Marie's health was failing and her daughter Edythe had become her partner. Marie passed away that year, and her sons bought the company, now Kuehmann Foods, a local giant with a full line of snack foods, more than 400 employees and its own truck fleet.

In May 1948, the company celebrated a $600,000 expansion and its 50th anniversary with a three-day open house and a special edition potato chip cookbook. An estimated 5,000 visitors toured the plant the first night. In this 50th anniversary photo, company officials and staff stand in front of the Kuehmann plant; Howard J. Nehrig, Jr., son of Kuehmann's local potato supplier, H.J. Nehrig, is fourth from the left. *Submitted by Ruth Nehrig, wife of Howard J. Nehrig, Jr.*

YOUNG APPRENTICES.

Leo Jarzynski was mustered out of the military in 1945. With an ill mother and no income, he had to forego the four years of college available under the G.I. Bill and look for a job. He was steered to a four-year die maker apprenticeship program with Doehler-Jarvis Co., a government-subsidized program that paid him $1.40 an hour while he learned. Here, in 1947, the apprentices gather for instruction at a large lathe at Macomber High School. By 1936, Doehler was the world's largest die casting producer. *Submitted by Leo and Christine Jarzynski.*

REMEMBER THE AQUARAMA.
Promoting Toledo as "the center of summer sports and frolic in the Maumee Valley Region" was the purpose of the Toledo Aquarama Festival. For 11 days in July and August, Toledo's Aquarama committee and the city parks department sponsored summer sports tournaments, parades and entertainment from water follies and canoe races to the Lady of the Lake beauty pageant, all at city parks and all free. In 1951, festival management was handed over to the city welfare department, which had implemented the festival in 1950. *Submitted by Ted Prisby.*

SIGN OF THE TIMES.
Wilbur Wiggam was quite the artist. Employed by Central Outdoor Advertising, Wilbur climbed his way atop many Toledo buildings to paint advertising billboards by hand. In 1947, the Schmidt Meats billboard topped the Hudson Furniture store near the corner of Detroit Avenue and Collingwood Blvd. The only building still in existence is the taller, Rosemary Apartments at the corner of Detroit and Phillips Avenues. *Submitted by Judy Pfaff, granddaughter of Wilbur.*

SERVICE AT ITS BEST.
Note the pristine white uniforms (including ties!) worn in the Jim White dealership's service department in 1949. Maynard "Joe" Marckel poses proudly under the "S" in Service, ninth man from the left in the back row. *Submitted by Naomi Davis.*

PUBLIC ART.
In the heydays for department stores, creating spectacular window displays was a true art form. The massive windows of Toledo's downtown stores – Lamson's, Lasalle's, Tiedtke's and Lion – were known for their imaginative displays. After the war, Robert Shifferly, at right in this 1948 snapshot, returned to his young wife, Joyce (Holderman) Shifferly, and was hired as assistant to Richard Kuhlman (left), Lamson's display manager. The display artists often traveled to Chicago and New York to buy materials and see displays created by the masters of the day. Kuhlman and Shifferly, who later built displays for Broer Freeman Jewelers, remained lifelong friends. *Submitted by Sandra Drake and Judith Holman.*

LEST WE FORGET.
Shown here is a United Veterans Memorial Day parade in 1949. The United Veterans Memorial Association members marching in this parade included Polish veterans, Catholic veterans, American Legion and VFW, all of the Lagrange Street area. The route of the parade was from Austin Street to Mt. Carmel Cemetery on Lagrange Street and Manhattan Boulevard, visible in the background. *Submitted by Christine Jarzynski.*

CLAIMS TO FAME.

The Toledo area Blue Cross Plan was established in 1938. In its first year, the new business enrolled more than 10,000 subscribers. Ten years later, Mary Ann Slowinski (third from left) was working at the Blue Cross Building at 448 Huron St., and they kept her busy. Within another ten years, the company had expanded from Lucas County to 11 counties in Ohio, enrolled 448,000 members (more than half the area's population), and paid more than $79 million in claims. *Submitted by Stephen and Mary Ann (Slowinski) Binkowski.*

LAKEFRONT TRANSFER FACILITY.

In this 1949 photograph, The Lakefront Dock & Railroad Terminal in Oregon Township, was in full operation moving domestic and foreign bulk commodities such as iron ore and coal through the Port of Toledo.

The facility covered 212 acres with 65 miles of railroad track and a total car capacity of 6,500, with a backup storage capacity of 7,000 cars.

The three coal dumpers were equipped to handle one car per minute each and were in service twenty-four hours daily year-round. Four Hulett ore machines, handling 60 tons every 60 seconds, transferred the ore from ship to cars. An electric pusher took over and pushed the car to a train of loaded cars, the first stage of its journey to one of the nation's steel mills.

In this photograph, the journey up these tracks was automated. The cars were pushed up the track by a barney to the cradle at the top. The cradle would level the car with the pan using cables to secure it in place. The pan would then tilt the entire railcar while lowering its spout, dumping the content into the ships hold. Once empty of their 60 ton cargo, the cars were

righted and sent down the other side. *Submitted by Jerry Schmuhl, retired supervisor of 35 years, and T.V. Mangan, retired superintendent of 20 years, The Lakefront Dock & Railroad Terminal Co., Port of Toledo.*

BEER BABE, 1950s STYLE.
Falstaff Beer, which had its beginnings in St. Louis in 1838, was the nation's seventh-largest brewer in the 1950s, producing more than two million barrels a year. Toledoan Jeannette Barba was a model for the company when Falstaff photographer Jim Patten snapped this shot, later used for a company billboard. After peaking at more than seven million barrels in the 1960s, Falstaff lost market share and in 2005, production ceased. *Submitted by Jeannette Barba Hurley.*

A GRANDPA FIRST.
Frank Lasko, known as "Whitey" to his family and friends, was an officiator at heart and a very busy man. After eight years as a deputy county clerk of courts, Mr. Lasko joined the county sheriff's department. He also served as a church trustee with St. Stephen's, a manager for the St. Emery Society baseball team and an active participant in Pee Wee League baseball. But, in this photo, Deputy Lasko has found time while on patrol in 1952 to stop by – on what must have been a very special "dress-up" kind of day – to see his granddaughter, Barbara. *Submitted by Barbara Bachar.*

PAINTING WITH THE STARS.
Chester Szymanski had no trouble filling the display windows at his hardware store at 320 North Hawley Street, especially with all the promotional material from Pittsburgh Paints. The campaign to sell their Wallhide products featured Garry Moore and Durward Kirby, stars of the wildly popular Garry Moore Show, and a contest to win $100,000. Garry Moore was the Johnny Carson of the 1950s and introduced viewers to some incredible talent, including Carol Burnett, Alan King and Candid Camera stunts. *Submitted by Chester R. Szymanski.*

ABOVE-GROUND POOL.
As World War II ended, the armed forces had a vast inventory of equipment they no longer needed . . . and an enormous war debt. W.C. VanGunten bought this inflatable lifeboat at the local Army-Navy surplus store in 1950 for his backyard at 1842 Sylvania Ave. The whole neighborhood enjoyed it including, from left, Laurie Goodremont, Carol Binkley, Roger VanGunten, Vincent Davie, and Sherrie Goodremont. (The Goodremont girls' father started the Goodremont office supply business in the home next door.) *Submitted by Roger VanGunten.*

TAKE ME OUT TO THE BALL GAME.
A rolling invitation to this 1950 Mud Hens game at Swayne Field was offered to all who would listen from The Gaylords. This barbershop bunch entertained the crowds at home games. The Gaylords are (backseat, left to right) Bill Deatrick (tenor), Charlie Coon (lead), Virgil Henry (baritone) and (front seat, left to right), Hal Counterman (lead) and Joe Bauer (bass). *Submitted by Paula Ashton, daughter of Bill Deatrick.*

HOOP DREAMS.
The Toledo Mercury basketball team traveled the country playing America's most famous basketball team, the Harlem Globetrotters. Owned by Toledoan Sid Goldberg, the team toured nationally from the late 1940s to the early 1960s. Sponsor Irv Pollock, a Lincoln-Mercury dealership owner, named the team and provided the team two Mercury automobiles for its tours. Pictured here in the dealership showroom on Monroe Street are, left to right, Sid Goldberg, Frank Sloan, Bobby Long, George Lingeman, Frank Gilhooley, Dick Mercer and Gene Hickey. *Submitted by Al Goldberg, son of Sid Goldberg.*

WHEN MEALS GOT WHEELS.

By the 1940s, America was in love with the automobile and drive-in restaurants were the next big thing for the newly mobile young and young-at-heart. Seen here as it was in the early 1950s, Don & Mel's Drive-in opened April 2, 1949, at Cherry Street and Delaware Avenue, adjacent to the existing Dairy Queen.

It was the first of many restaurants Don Baumgartner and Mel Berman would build separately over the years. By 1961 Baumgartner had five popular Don's Drive-ins in Toledo and Maumee. Mel Berman went on to build his own local retail empire with Frostop Drive-ins, Mel's Big Burgers, Mel Berman's restaurant, Chris Berman's Supper Club and the Toledo 5 Unocal truck stop off the Ohio Turnpike, as well as Berman's Christmas & Gift Shoppe and Berman's Flower Shoppe. *Submitted by Douglas Baumgartner, son of Don Baumgartner.*

GOOD EATS AT EPPES ESSEN.

Eppes Essen – Yiddish for "something to eat" – was one of downtown Toledo's Jewish delis from its opening in the 1940s until it closed some 40 years later. In this photo from the 1950s, owner Lily Levinson is shown with her sons Sid, left, and Manny, right. *Submitted by Rebecca Walsh, daughter of Manny.*

THE STARS CAME OUT.

The city of Toledo was booming in 1950, and the results of its prosperity could be found everywhere, especially in the transportation industry. The opening of Toledo's new Union Station was celebrated with an entire week of parades and performances. All the Hollywood studios sent their top celebrities to the festivities, including ingénue actress Mitzi Gaynor (waving to the crowd), age 19, from 20th Century Fox; William Holden from Paramount; Marta Torin from Universal Studios, Western star Tim Holt from RKO Pictures and George Murphy from M-G-M, as well as TV star and native son Danny Thomas. *Submitted by Mary Ann and Stephen Binkowski.*

IT'S THE REAL THING.

Owner Simon Njaim smiles proudly in front of the display window of the Delux Carry Out, circa 1950. His popular neighborhood establishment, located at the corner of Norwood and Upton Avenues, obviously was a strong proponent of Coca-Cola. *Submitted by Melissa Callejas, granddaughter of Simon Njaim.*

LET'S BOWL.
These young ladies, photographed circa 1950, were members of bowling teams at Toledo Scale. At that time, the company employed about 3,000 Toledoans. The two lanes pictured in this unidentified bowling alley had no automatic ball returns or pin setters. *Submitted by Corrine Gauthier, seated fifth from the left.*

GET YOUR OWN RIDE.
Toledo's own Willys-Overland Motors, Inc., was one of Toledo's industrial leaders as its trademark defense product, the Jeep, was becoming popular domestically. Selecting the busy intersection of Central Avenue and Monroe Street to display their product was a smart choice. In the 1950s, many families experienced owning their very first automobile. *Submitted by Judy Pfaff.*

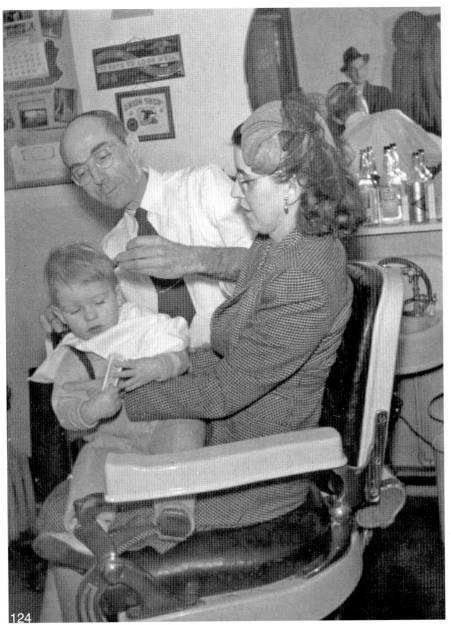

GREENGROCER.
Before truck peddlers were affected by the dominance of supermarkets, Bob Kaufman, far right, sold fruits and vegetables from his mobile market in the Old West End and in South Toledo. This photo of Bob, with an unknown man at left and Grant Gose, center, was taken in September, 1949 – just as the apple harvest was coming in. *Submitted by Helen Kaufman, wife of Bob Kaufman.*

JUST A LITTLE OFF THE TOP, PLEASE.
A first haircut is an experience to be celebrated – if you're the parent. This anxious tot is Tom Lancaster, Jr., sitting on the lap of his mother, Betty Lancaster, in 1952. (Let's hope she held him still – those scissors look like they could hurt someone). *Submitted by Judy Pfaff, daughter of Betty and sister of Tom.*

MIKE'S DAD.
John Manion is captured on film as he's leaving his Bancroft Street home, just steps from Auburn Avenue. Once a primarily residential neighborhood, the houses across the street from the Manion residence are now gone. *Submitted by Mike Manion, son of John Manion.*

STANDING ROOM ONLY.
This eager crowd, mostly boys, is participating in a "Pie Eater's Club" event sponsored by B. R. Baker's clothing store. The young people in this photograph are waiting to attend an ice show at the Sports Arena about 1950. (Note the Deco chandeliers in the lobby). *Submitted by Dolores Eberly.*

A ROAD WELL-TRAVELED.
The Berdan and Jeep Parkway intersection was the gateway to Toledo's automotive empire at Willys-Overland. The brilliant billboards in this late 1940s photo spotlight vehicles that were an integral part of the lifeblood of Toledo's economy. The modern day Jeep is still one of America's useful vehicles (as the billboard raves) and maintains its place in the economy of the city. *Submitted by Judy Pfaff.*

BODY MAN.
Richard Wilkinson, a body repairman for Roth Pontiac, is pictured here in the repair shop. This photo was taken in 1951; Richard worked there a total of 30 years. *Photo submitted by Linda Wing, daughter of Richard Wilkinson.*

FUNNY FARM.
In the early 1950s, local television stations produced a variety of programming. One children's show, Fun Farm with Mary Ellen, ran for three years in Toledo on WSPD and for two years in Cleveland on WEWS. Kids from around the area would be on the show, and there were coloring contests and opportunities to win prizes. Mary Ellen entertained with marionettes, and a mounted policeman would ride his horse into the studio to sing. A former art student, Mary Ellen also would draw caricatures of the children using their initials in a segment she called "Funny Face." *Submitted by Judy Pfaff.*

TOLEDO EXPRESS.
Norman Witherell couldn't wait for Toledo's new airport to be completed before he grabbed this snapshot in early 1954. Toledo Express Airport was completed without the aid of state or federal funds, costing nearly $3.9 million. An estimated 35,000 attended the dedication October 31, 1954. The first inbound flight, a Lockheed Lodestar that landed January 5 around 7:30 p.m., went largely unnoticed – all flights had been cancelled that day due to low visibility. So most official records name the Capital Airlines flight from Detroit, arriving at 8:30 a.m. the next morning, as the first to land. *Submitted by Ron Westphal, grandson of Norman Witherell.*

PUMPED UP FOR BUSINESS.
Proud manager Emery Mate (standing), known as "Jim" to friends, looks out the glass wall of his new Sinclair service station at Front and Consaul streets in 1951. (His friend, seated, is unidentified.) Jim and son-in-law Richard Langel, who worked at the station, lived in the Birmingham neighborhood and often ate lunch across the street at Tony Packo's. Tony's older brother, Robert, is credited with taking this photo. Today, this is the site of Tony Packo's Central Kitchen. *Submitted by Carolyn (Langel) Carr, granddaughter of Emery Mate.*

JACK OF ALL TRADES.
Leroy Hardnett takes a break in this circa 1951 photo. Leroy owned several businesses in his lifetime: Leroy's Market on Norwood and Smead, Ellis Ambulance Service, a UHaul service, Leroy's Towing and American Cab Company. *Submitted by LaRoyna (Hardnett) Drayton, daughter of Leroy Hardnett.*

BIRTH OF THE SUV.
These Willys crankshaft workers in 1951 were part of automotive history. Having won fame for its hard-working "Jeep" vehicle during World War II, Willys-Overland continued to build Jeeps and expanded its line to meet increasing demand for harder-working vehicles here at home. Willys-Overland started building Willys Wagons in 1949 with a workhorse six-cylinder engine and four-wheel drive, and the "sport utility vehicle" was born. Two years later, the company was sold to Kaiser and became the Willys Motor Company. *Submitted by Candace Kluender, wife of John Kluender (behind the man in the front row wearing the cap with his hand on his shoulder).*

A BRAND NEW CAR!
Ed Sullivan's television variety show, "Taste of the Town," was enormously popular and he made numerous appearances for charity. Appearing at the Toledo Sports, Home, Food and Auto Show in 1951, Sullivan also acted as master of ceremonies for a luncheon hosted by two automotive dealers who sponsored his show locally – Irv Pollock, Inc. and Bauer-Harrington, Inc. After presenting a station wagon on their behalf to the Toledo Council of Social Agencies, Mr. Sullivan magnanimously announced he was now giving away 300 automobiles. A parade of shapely young ladies then marched in with enough model cars on trays for everyone in attendance. *Submitted by Bill Wyatt.*

GET YOUR MOTORS RUNNIN'.
This sharp photograph shows clearly the faces of these Willys-Overland workers in 1952. They were employed in the section that assembled motor blocks. Joe Hanley is seated third from the left. (The gentleman in the front row with the shirt and tie seems out of place). *Submitted by Joseph P. Hanley II.*

POLISH PRIDE.
Quite a crowd is gathered to watch this Polish band, headed by five trombones, march down the street, probably on Memorial Day, circa 1953. Steinman Auto Repair, seen at the far left, was at 211-219 Ontario Street. The band is parading north, most likely to the courthouse. *Submitted by Ted Kanapek and Dorothy Mioduszczewski.*

FROM THE TOP, NOW.
The interior of Western Avenue Methodist Church is shown in this 1950s photograph with Rev. Melvin Grossman standing behind a young choir. The church building at 1501 Western Avenue had obviously bocomo crowdcd, and latcr thc congregation joined Somerset United Brethren to form New Hope Church. *Submitted by Marilee Taylor, archivist of New Hope United Methodist.*

HAPPY TO BE HOME.
U.S. Marine Corporal Richard Stewart, 22, smiles outside Toledo's Union Station in 1952 as family members welcome him home after more than a year in hospitals recovering from battle wounds received in Korea. A Purple Heart recipient, Richard was one of three Stewart brothers serving in Korea at the same time: brother Harold also was wounded, and Raymond, Jr. was drafted in 1951. Family and friends here are, from left, uncle Russell Stewart (far left), Richard, friends Lil Dukeshire and baby Deborah, father Raymond (back to camera), sister Doris Stewart and mother Edna. *Submitted by Doris (Stewart) Lynch.*

TAKING A BREAK.
Brantley Merwell "Fritz" Pifer (top row second from left) takes a break with his workmates at The Spicer Manufacturing Company plant on Bennett Road. Mr. Pifer came to Toledo, following his older brother James, from rural southern Illinois (Barnhill) in 1937 because of the availability of work in the "Auto Parts Capital of the World." Like many others, he did find work. He also found Mary Lou Benner. They married, reared a family and he spent the remainder of his life in Toledo. The Spicer plant moved to Toledo from New Jersey in 1928 as a manufacturer of gears and axels for trucks and buses. Later, as a part of the Dana Corporation, the company was one of a number of Toledo plants making automobile parts and accessories and employed as many as 4,000 people. Others included AP Parts, Electric Auto-Lite and Champion Spark Plug. By the 1960s the Spicer plant had diversified its product line which included truck transmissions, and universal joints as well as parts for aircraft and railroad locomotives. Production ceased there in the late 1980s and the facility, which still stands, was purchased by the Willis Day Storage Company. *Submitted by Sandy and John R. Husman, daughter and son-in-law of Fritz Pifer.*

IT'S A GOOD LIFE.

Those who know say it takes a strong marriage for spouses to work together as well as live together. That's obviously true for Tony and Rose Packo, who had been married 18 years when this photo was taken in 1945. Rose is perched on Tony's lap and mugging for the camera, probably after closing the restaurant for the night, in the kitchen of their living quarters behind the restaurant at Front and Consaul streets. The two had opened the restaurant in 1932. *Submitted by Tony Packo, Jr., son of Tony and Rose Packo.*

CLOSED FOR A CELEBRATION.

Tony Packo's restaurant at Front and Consaul streets closed only once, and on a Saturday, no less: the day of daughter Nancy's wedding. The "customers" along this bar are family and friends attending the reception, held in the restaurant. The too-young-for-a-barstool gentleman in the foreground is relative Paul Kovacs, Jr., whose father worked part-time for the restaurant. *Submitted by Tony Packo, Jr., son of Tony and Rose Packo.*

WAITE TWIRLERS.

The Waite High School majorettes of 1953 pose outside the school's magnificent stadium, one of only three built in Ohio with walls on all sides. They are, from left, Kay Christie, Elizabeth Szor, Elaine Layman, Shirley Sawade, Alice Palmiter, Betty Shaffer, Joyce Heider and Lou Ann Gibbons. *Submitted by 1954 Waite H.S. graduate Alice (Palmiter) Evanoff.*

RAMBLING MAN.
Ford Miller, a Nash Motors dealer, and Bill Wyatt, District Manager for Universal Commercial Investment Trust, are sitting high in a 1902 Rambler automobile in May of 1953. The Ford Miller Motors Inc. showroom was located at 1127 Washington Street. Miller Motors also included a body shop at 1119 Washington Street and a used car division at 1202 Washington Street. *Submitted by Bill Wyatt.*

SINGING SUPERSTAR.
The dark-haired gentleman at the microphone is internationally known recording star and actor Don Cornell, who visited Toledo in 1953 for two daily appearances at the Home and Builder's Show at the Sports Arena. He was also a guest on Art Barrie's WSPD radio show. Mr. Cornell, born Luigi Varlaro in the Bronx, recorded with the Coral, Dot, Fox Movietone and ABC Paramount labels. He became one of the top big band singers of the 1950s and was honored with one of the first stars on the Hollywood Walk of Fame. *Submitted by Corinne Gauthier.*

READY AND WAITING.

Sitting on the curb and waiting for a parade in downtown Toledo in 1953 are, from left, Sue, Bobby and Nancy Ellithorpe, and Kathleen and Seto You. Mr. You, originally from Canton, China, came to this area in the early 1920s. He worked as a chef in a variety of restaurants and met his wife, Mary, at one of the restaurants where she worked as a dishwasher. He later owned and operated Kin Wa Low's, a Chinese restaurant and nightclub. They had four children, including young Kathleen, and lived above the restaurant. *Submitted by Kathleen You Johnson and Wayne You, children of Seto You.*

DRAWING A CROWD.

The date is May 24, 1953, and this crowd has gathered at the corner of Walnut and Superior Streets for the dedication of the new education building of Holy Trinity Greek Orthodox Cathedral. Part of the church, built in 1920, can be seen across Walnut Street at upper right. Walnut Street to the right has since been closed to become part of the parish grounds, as has Superior to the south of the intersection, now a parking lot. The parish, which has 450 families, is an important presence in the near north end neighborhood of Vistula. *Submitted by Rev. Aristotle Damaskos, Holy Trinity Greek Orthodox Cathedral.*

CRUISING ON THE CREEK.

As soon as spring weather settled in, Richard Turnow (at wheel), his brother-in-law Carl Kutz and their families would head for their cabins along a creek near Maumee Bay. Here, young Robert Kutz (left) and big brother Fred are along for a ride with uncle Rich. The boys' parents, Carl and Gladys (Turnow) Kutz, were raised on farms, and the cabin was a welcome rural retreat from the bustle of the city. Dwight D. Eisenhower, an avid outdoorsman, is said to have visited a small hunting cabin nearby during his presidency. *Submitted by Fred Kutz.*

A FAMILY AFFAIR.

Many neighborhoods in Toledo during the 1950s were peppered with mom and pop corner stores and cafes. Logan's Carryout on the corner of Douglas Road and Arletta Street was owned by William and Pauletta Logan. The Logan family lived behind and above the store. The older Logan kids helped mom and dad operate the store, which was quite a feat since dad William worked full time at Spicer Manufacturing Company. This photo taken in 1954 catches Ivan Logan (in the flannel shirt) and his father-in-law holding down the fort. The Logans ran the carryout from the early 1950s until 1960. *Submitted by Anne (Logan) Ewing*

READY, SET, GO!

John Connors poses atop the car he built himself in the summer of 1954. Made of two orange crates and an old wagon, it was painted cherry red. Note the upholstery: two pillows. *Submitted by John Connors.*

A RARE OPPORTUNITY.

Alice Palmiter (later Evanoff), 17, and friend Bernie Westfall smile in a Woodill Wildfire in front of the Rivoli Theater in 1954. One of only a handful made, the Wildfire was an all-American-parts sports car built in 1952 with Toledo-made Willys engine parts and a lightweight Glasspar body by B.R. "Woody" Woodill, a successful Dodge dealer. The Wildfire is considered by car aficionados to be the birth of production of American fiberglass sports cars.

Willys plans to produce the Wildfire fell through when Kaiser Frazer bought Willys. Looking for another automaker, Woodill promoted the Wildfire by featuring it in four films, including *Johnny Dark*, the film promoted on the car, starring Tony Curtis and Piper Laurie. *Submitted by Alice (Palmiter) Evanoff.*

A LOT OF GREEN.

This aerial view shows the extensive Hirzel Greenhouse operation at the corner of Oregon and Wales Roads in August 1954. Alfred and Sophie Hirzel started the business in 1922 with 15 greenhouses. Later, ten more greenhouses were moved from Miami Street and six others added on two additional acres to make 31 greenhouses in all. The familiar Hirzel smokestack on the boiler house was 105 feet tall. At first, cucumbers were grown, but later the only crops were lettuce from September to December and tomatoes from February to July. The operation used 40 rail cars of coal a year. Sons Alfred A. and Walter R. Hirzel were brought in as partners in 1942. Nothing is left of the four and one-half acres under glass at the busy intersection of Oregon and Wales Roads today. *Submitted by Robert Hirzel.*

UNION SCALE.

Sitting pretty aboard this Toledo Scale float in Toledo's 1954 Labor Day Parade are, left to right, Nancy Lapinski, Dee Lendecker (Slowinski) and Barbara Main. The float represented Local 773 of the UAW – CIO. The first Labor Day celebration took place in New York City in 1882. On June 28, 1894, Congress passed an act making the first Monday in September of each year a legal holiday in the District of Columbia and the territories. *Submitted by Dolores Slowinski.*

SITTING PRETTY.

A visit to the Toledo Zoo just wasn't complete without at least one ride on the miniature train. Little Barbara Varkoly, age 5, must have been first in line. She has already taken her seat and waits patiently while other children climb aboard. The Toledo Zoo has thrilled children with its miniature trains since 1946. The train seen here was a steam-powered locomotive built to scale, put in operation in 1950 after then-mayor Michael V. DiSalle (later Ohio governor) drove in the golden spike that completed its construction. *Submitted by Barbara (Varkoly) Bachar.*

THE HORSE KNOWS THE WAY.

As late as 1955, Charlie the horse still pulled a milk wagon for Sealtest Dairy in Toledo. Here he waits patiently at the corner while Finley Johnston finishes making his deliveries to front-porch milk boxes. Charlie would not have to wait very long, however, for the end of the horse-drawn milk wagon era. *Submitted by Mike Johnston.*

DANCING AT TEEN TOWN.

For junior high and high school students from Blissfield to Tiffin and beyond, the Teen Town dances were THE places to be. Teen Town members had everything from bowling parties to charity drives from 1945 to the 70s. Hopewell School at Jackman and Alexis roads was the site of this Teen Town dance in 1955. Gathered at the Wishing Well are (from left) Bob Steinmetz, Sharon Meck, Dave Korn, Pat Riley, Ed Korn, Bob Bartel, Bonna Bergman, Joyce Pack and Judy Raitz. *Submitted by Joyce Pack.*

YOU SAY TOMATO.

Wright Brothers Wholesale Gardeners had over 13 acres of hothouse tomatoes under glass in 1952. The sprawling $1.5 million business was located on Bancroft, between Cheltenham and University Circle, as seen in this overhead photo taken from The University of Toledo tower. *Submitted by Kevin Kubiak.*

TARZAN IN THE MAKING?
Bob Richards, 12, swings in the gym at the Boys Club on Superior Street near Cherry in 1955. The facility was built in 1911 for the Toledo Newsboys Association, founded in 1892 by local railroad ticket agent John Gunckel to help area newsboys (often homeless) become productive citizens. The Newsboys sponsored educational and social activities including the Newsboys Marching Band, which performed in the parade for President Theodore Roosevelt's inauguration in 1905. The Toledo Newsboys officially became the Boys Club of Toledo in 1942 and changed to the Boys & Girls Club in the 1980s. *Submitted by Bob Richards.*

LIKE MY NEW RIDE?
Large exhibits were nothing new for Walbridge Park, the place that gave birth to The Toledo Zoo. So it was a natural choice for a display of planes, tanks and a carrier to celebrate Armed Forces Day in 1952. It was an exciting day for Mike Manion (left), age 12, and cousin John Mack, 10, who not only posed with the plane, but were allowed to climb all over the equipment. *Submitted by Mike Manion.*

A BEAUTY OF AN EDUCATION.
The original Notre Dame Academy stood on West Bancroft Street between Forest and Horace streets. The Notre Dame nuns purchased the land in 1902, part of the Outing Park Addition owned by Thomas Walbridge, who had served on the Toledo board of park commissioners. (Horace Street was named for Walbridge's father, local businessman Horace S. Walbridge, also the namesake for Toledo's Walbridge Park.) The school opened in 1904 and graduated its first class of two students soon thereafter. It was demolished in 1960 for construction of a hotel/motel. *Submitted by Corrine Gauthier.*

SAY CHEESE.
John and Jeff Rutter are "udderly" spellbound by *Bossy*, the cow on display at the Toledo Zoo's Wonder Valley, July 1955. Many children visited the zoo to milk *Bossy*, or ride on *Galopy*, the giant tortoise (see page 150). *Submitted by Tom Rutter.*

LUNCH WITH A LEGEND.
Sharon Lei Manore was just 14 when a new rock-n-roll star named Elvis Presley performed two Thanksgiving Day shows at the Sports Arena in 1956. Tickets were $2 and $2.50. Sharon's essay won a radio promotion; her prize was lunch with Elvis. After the second show, Mr. Presley escaped to the Commodore Perry Hotel, where he was attacked by a local man shouting that his recently estranged wife carried a photo of Elvis but not her own husband. Miss Manore, an 8th grader at Longfellow Elementary, predicted that Elvis would be "a famous singer for a very long time to come." *Submitted by Sharon Lei's mother, Evelyn Manore.*

ALONG THE WATERFRONT.

This skyline view of the downtown waterfront shows how far Toledo had come by 1956. Evidently, local homebuilder Robert Schroeder was impressed; he took this photo from his boat during a cruise up the Maumee River. *Submitted by Linda (Schroeder) Sepanski, daughter of Robert Schroeder.*

MEET THE CONGREGATION.

On October 7, 1956, the congregation of Somerset Evangelical United Brethren Church sat for this formal photo inside their church at 2025 Wayne Street. Since most of the children are seated together, it's believed this photo was taken during Somerset's Rally Days celebration, which signals the start of a new year of Bible School. Somerset later merged with Western Avenue Methodist to become New Hope Methodist Church. *Submitted by Marilee Taylor, archivist of New Hope United Methodist.*

EVERYONE IN THE POOL!

Everyone had a few "good words" for the secretarial typing pool at the Toledo Testing Labs on North 12th Street – and these women made sure each word was entered properly. Patty Dempsey can be seen at her desk in the lower left corner of this 1956 photo. *Submitted by Pamela (Dempsey) Sample.*

AS FRESH AS IT GETS.

William Zouhary, owner of the former Sherbrooke Restaurant, still prepared his trademark Caesar salad fresh at the table for customers in 1964. He learned the secrets of making Caesar salad (named for Italian chef/restaurateur Caesar Cardini) directly from Chef Pierre at the Taft Hotel Grill in Manhattan's theater district.

The Sherbrooke operated from 1953 to 1969, with sons Tom and Bill helping on weekends. The building later housed other exceptional restaurants including the El Greco and, today, the Beirut. *Submitted by Tom Zouhary, son of William Zouhary.*

OOOPS!

The Cleveland Cliffs freighter *Champlain* is shown here after ramming the Fassett Street Bridge in this 1957 photo. A severe storm with winds up to 90 miles per hour broke the 620-foot ship loose from its moorings, and it was blown downriver into the old bridge. The bridge operator was in the building at the time, but luckily the ship was deflected away from the swing span at the last moment. The west end of the bridge was destroyed, the third and last time a part of the bridge had fallen into the water. It was not considered worth rebuilding, and by 1960 the whole bridge had been dismantled. *Submitted by Connie Warner and Harold Mucci.*

PLAID'S THE FAD.

Long before George Lucas filmed *American Graffiti*, Peggy Allen, Helen Campbell and Glenda Corbitt enjoyed their own good times in front of Mel's Drive-In. The air is crisp on this April day in 1956, so they're wearing their winter best. *Submitted by Olivia Holden.*

HAPPY HOLIDAYS.
This 1958 photo of a group of Willys-Overland workers shows that work in one department was stopped for a little holiday fun as they pose by a chalk-drawn picture of Santa. *Submitted by Evelyn Oswald Buchholtz.*

GIVE THANKS.
The year was 1957, and there was plenty to be thankful for. At the Bigland house on Poinsettia Street, kids Bob and Pat patiently lined up for a piece of the Thanksgiving turkey, while dad Robert carved. Mom, known as "Babe," waited for hers, too, while baby Jim wondered what that was on his plate. *Submitted by Jim Bigland.*

THEY CAME FROM OUTER SPACE.

The Space Race was on by the late 1950s, reflected in popular culture everywhere, including Calvin M. Woodward High School in 1959. This stage number was developed for the Woodward majorettes as a half-time show, inspired by then-popular novelty songs including Sheb Wooley's "One-Eyed, One-Horned Flying Purple People Eater" by the Big Bopper. The "aliens" on the bottom row, from left, are Sandra London, Joanne Saba, Helen Charney and Judy Sorge. Top row, from left: Sue Downey, Barbara Wichowski, Judy Jokinen (costumer designer) and Jane McGee. *Submitted by Judy (Jokinen) Nickoloff.*

KEEPING THE PRESSES ROLLING.

In this photo from the 1950s, *Blade* pressmen (from left) Robert Van Scoy, Stanley Filipowicz, Ralph Fata, Phillip Kinney and Norman Hassinger share a light moment. Note their traditional pressmen's hats. The press is by Goss – the same manufacturer that made the presses *The Blade* uses today. *Submitted by Micaela Maxwell.*

KING FOR A DAY.
The famous comedian from Toledo, Joe E. Brown, is being honored in this parade down Lagrange Street in 1958. Mr. Brown is seated on the car, facing the camera and wearing the interesting hat. He is on the way to the dedication of the park to be named in his honor. Joe E. Brown, known for his wide mouth, was a very well-known comic in his day and one of Toledo's most famous entertainers, along with Danny Thomas and, later, Jamie Farr. *Submitted by Christine Jarzynski.*

THE BEARS ARE COMING.
During the WWII years, The Toledo Zoo's explosive expansion thanks to the WPA came to a halt. After 1950, it began anew. The post-war "baby boom" and economic recovery boosted the Zoo's attendance to an estimated one million visitors a year. Construction began with a new miniature railroad in 1950, then continued to include an expanded parking lot, the bar-free bear grotto (seen here in its early stage) and the petting zoo and family favorite, Wonder Valley. The Zoo hired Ned Skeldon as its first full-time, salaried director in 1953. *Submitted by longtime Zoo members Mary Ann and Stephen Binkowski.*

QUEEN JANET THE FIRST.
On Thanksgiving Day, 1958, Janet Quinn prepares to walk on the football field proudly holding the title of Scott High School's first African-American Homecoming Queen. The Scott Bull Dogs beat Waite 6-0, making the victory even sweeter! *Submitted by Janet (Quinn) Wyatt.*

PERCHED IN THE AVIARY.
From the 1940s on, Mary Ann and Stephen Binkowski found that a membership to The Toledo Zoo was just the ticket for their large family. The Binkowskis visited on average once a month, with nine children and picnic baskets in tow. In this 1958 photo in the Aviary, Richard, age 5, perches on the railing in fascination while sister Lisa, 3, looks on. Built with WPA funds and material salvaged from other demolished Zoo buildings, the Aviary included the first known use of structural glass block walls (visible in the background), donated by Owens-Illinois. A few years later, another innovation would arrive: the elephant key and Talking Storybooks. *Submitted by Mary Ann and Stephen Binkowski.*

AHEAD OF OUR TIME.
In the 1950s, downtown stores everywhere began losing shoppers to suburban shopping centers. In the summer of 1959, Toledo experimented with the concept of downtown pedestrian malls. One was along Adams Street, another on Madison Avenue. Here, the stretch of Adams Street in front of Lasalle's Department Store has had a total transformation, with flowing paved walkways and decorative plantings. *Submitted by Peggy Kirk.*

HIGHER, HIGHER!
For two months, traffic was rerouted around these shopping areas and the streets were filled with children's playground equipment, flowerbeds, performers, decorations and benches for weary shoppers. The playgrounds, of course, were wildly popular. Here, Jimmy Kirk, 3, and Peggy Kirk, 6, are having a great time on the glider in front of the B.R. Baker Co. store. *Submitted by Peggy Kirk.*

A BOWSER "DOGPILE"
Another playground area was installed in front of the F.W. Woolworth store. The Bowser children are burning off pent-up energy here: (from top) Bill, Larry, Kathy, Dave and Steve. Civic leaders and shoppers from around the country gave Toledo's pedestrian mall rave reviews. Participating stores reported significant sales increases. But the idea was tabled after the experiment. Since then, pedestrian malls have been implemented successfully in many mid-sized and larger cities around the country. *Submitted by Kathy (Bowser) Klausing.*

READY TO PLAY.

For many years, Corey Road Field, between Central and Sylvania Avenues, was the site of vigorous polo matches. John E. "Jack" Hankison (on horse) prepares for a match at Corey Road Field in 1960 as fans assemble on and around their cars to watch. Mr. Hankison was a very active member of the Springbrook Polo Club from 1953 through the 1960s, scheduling matches with polo clubs locally and throughout the region. *Submitted by Carol (Hillebrand) Arnold, niece of John E. Hankison.*

PROUD OF THEIR WORK.

These workers at Dura Corporation gather among the pulleys and machinery for this picture in October 1959. They were members of regular assembly section three. Dura Corporation was originally part of the Detroit Harvester Company, and by the time of this photo Dura Division of Dura Corporation manufactured auto parts and accessories at 4500 Detroit Avenue. *Submitted by Irene Lindsey.*

"SMOOTH LIKE BUTTA."
Tiedtke's bakery counter brings back good gastronomic memories to Toledoans who remember shopping there. This circa 1959 photo shows Elizabeth Wood, Ruth Welling, Bob Kuchnicki and an unidentified lady on the right touting their delicious butter cookies. The master baker at Tiedtke's for many years was Louis Heilbrun, now in his 90s, who still remembers many of his famous recipes. *Submitted by Louis and Vern Heilbrun.*

OPEN FOR BUSINESS.
Previously pastureland within Hasty Hill Farm, the new Westgate shopping center at Secor Road and Central Avenue — not yet within the city limits — opened in 1957 with plenty of fanfare. It was billed as having everything "for the modern Toledo." The ceremonies were televised and included a drawing for a two-week European trip, music by Vaughan Monroe and his orchestra (on the platform above the arcade entrance), and an appearance by TV personality Denise Lor from the very popular Garry Moore Show. Soon thereafter, despite a legal battle that went all the way to the state supreme court, Toledo annexed a portion of Washington Township, including the shopping center. *Submitted by Louise Holland, daughter of Westgate developer Joseph J. Abbell.*

SLOW DOWN, WILL YA?

It was slow going in the children's area of the Toledo Zoo, *Wonder Valley*, when Peggy Ehrsham (Roberts) took her turn riding the giant tortoise, Galopy, in the summer of 1960. She wasn't scared; Grandma Harriet Walbolt stood close by, but a little guy behind her looks a little anxious for his turn. Wonder Valley opened in May of 1953 and covered two acres introducing children to the joy of animals. It featured ponds, windmills, and at its peak – contained over 100 animals. In 1983, it was renamed the Children's Zoo, and was replaced and relocated to a larger site. *Submitted by Winona Collier, Peggy's mom.*

LITTLE CAR, BIG WINNER.

By the 1960s, America's passion for speed had been running rampant for well over 30 years. Starting in California in the 1930s, midget racing spread quickly across the country and soared in popularity after World War II. Toledo was a hotbed of midget racing activity. Barry Coop, 11, seen here in 1960 in his midget racer at Scott Park's racetrack, and his brothers were completely absorbed in it, racing at the Lucas County Recreation Center, Scott Park and occasionally out of town. Joe Slowinski, Barry's uncle, often helped the boys build and maintain their racers. *Submitted by Stephen and Mary Ann (Slowinski) Binkowski, uncle and aunt of Barry Coop.*

TRAGIC PLANE CRASH.

On October 29, 1960, this Arctic Pacific airplane carrying the 16 members of the Cal Poly San Luis Obispo football team crashed on takeoff at the Toledo Express Airport. It was one of the worst sport team disasters ever in this country. Of the 48 people aboard, 22 died. It is believed that the plane lost power in engine No. 1 and may have exceeded its weight limit. Tom Wodarski, employed by Eastern Airlines in Toledo at the time, obtained these rare photographs just after the tragic accident. (Notice the book among the debris in the inset, enlarged from the foreground of the top photo). *Submitted by Tom Wodarski.*

HOMECOMING QUEEN.

Sharon Goldie, Scott High School's 1960 Homecoming Queen, smiles from the back of a convertible as she waits for the festivities to begin. She would later attend Fisk College, where she would be crowned queen of her freshman class. *Submitted by Frank Goldie, father of Sharon Goldie.*

WELL DONE, WELBORN.

Todd Welborn, 2, concentrates intently on grilling the perfect burger in 1960. This little grill sergeant did not grow up to be a famous chef. Instead he served 21 years in the U.S. Army – completing his career as a Special Forces medic. He continues to enjoy barbecuing and is still trying to perfect his grilling skills. *Submitted by Sara Welborn, his favorite sister, and Jane Bryan Welborn, his mother.*

SUBJECT INDEX

A
AAA 55
Adams Street 12, 29, 39, 42, 55, 70, 84, 89, 113, 147
Adkins, E.H. Grocery Store 43
Advance Glove 85
Airline Avenue 17
Airport Highway 64
Airports 51, 93, 126, 151
Albion Street 112
Alexis Road 137
All Saints Episcopal Church 57
American Cab Company 127
American District Telegraph 58
American Express 7
American Flint Glass Workers 22
American Graffiti 142
American Legion 117
American League 109
American Shipbuilding Company 40, 104
Amusement parks 8, 15, 32, 33, 42, 46, 52
Ann Page Foods 71
Anthony Wayne Bridge (High Level) 56; Trail 30
A & P 71
AP Parts 130
Apprenticeships 115
Aquarama Festival 116
Aranyosi's Studio 79
Arctic II 99
Arctic Pacific airplane 151
Arletta Street 134
Arlington Avenue 45
Armed Forces Day 138
Armories 5, 11
Armory Park 11
Army-Navy Surplus 120
Auburn Avenue 25
Auburndale 9
Austin Street 117
Autolite (see Electric Auto-Lite)
Avenue Café 76
Avondale Street 4

B
B&L Bar 103
Baker, B.R. 29, 55, 88, 125, 147
Bakeries 82, 102, 113
Bancroft Street 43, 50, 125, 138
Barney 17
Bars 2, 22, 26, 103
Baseball 44, 50, 71, 87, 89, 109, 114, 119
Basketball 22, 62, 120
Bathing 17, 37, 46, 52,
Battle of the Bulge 102
Bay View Park 28, 83
Beirut, The 141
Belle Isle 8
Berdan Avenue 125
Berger's cider mill 71
Big Bopper 144
Birmingham neighborhood 16, 58
Blade, The building, back cover; carriers 66, 75, pressmen 144
Blacksmiths 12
Black Tuesday 63
Blue Cross 118
Bob's Grill 103
Bohemia 7
Booth Red Sox 71
Bowling alleys 16, 123
Bowling Green 23
Boxing 28, 89
Boy Scouts 106
Boys Club 138
Boys & Girls Club 138
Braatz Moving and Storage Company 40
Breweries 26, 74, 103, 114
Bridge Street 1
Bridges 18, 30, 45, 46; Anthony Wayne (High Level) 56; Ash-Consaul 13; Cherry Street 8, 13, 19; Fassett Street 142; Glendale Avenue 30; South Street 45
Broadway 2, 4, 15, 27, 35, 53, 103
Broadway View Bar 2
Broer Freeman Jewelers 117
Brooklyn Dodgers 109
Brown, Joe E. 145
Brown Avenue 82
Brown Road 49
Brownies 92
Buckingham Street 62
Buffalo Street 22
Bunting Brass and Bronze 46
Byrne Road 45

C
California gold rush 8
Cal Poly San Luis Obispo football team 151
Camp Libbey 54
Camp Miakonda 106
Camp Perry Training Site 21
Canals 26, 30, 97
Canton Avenue 11, 76
Capitol Airlines 126
Casinos 15, 26
Cass Road 42
Castle Boulevard 42
Caesar salad 141
Cedar Point 32, 33, 52, 53; Beach 112; Cyclone 32
Cemeteries 18, 26, 61, 117
Central Avenue 19, 123, 148, 149
Central Catholic High School 53
Central High School 39
Central Labor Union Building 113
Central Outdoor Advertising 116
Chamber of Commerce 108
Champion Spark Plug 116, 130
Champlain 142
Chase Bag Co., 82
Chase Street 20
Cheltenham 137
Cherry School 42
Cherry Street 5, 38, 98, 101, 111, 138
Cherry Street Bridge 8
Chillicothe 26
Chinese Relief Association 110
Chippewa tribe 14
Chippewa Golf Course 14
Christen, Fred & Sons 113
Christmas party 114, trees 102, 107
Churches 1, 2, 4, 35, 43, 49, 57, 58, 92, 93
"Cinderella" 78
Circus 94
Citizen's Ice Company 86
City Park 33, 57
Civic Mall 112
Civil War 32
Civil War veterans 1, 10, 15, 24
Cleveland Ordnance District 95
Cleveland Indians 109
Collingwood Boulevard 15, 43, 75, 86, 116
Collingwood Methodist Episcopal Church 92
Collins Park 50
Comedians Joe E. Brown 145, Danny Thomas 122, 145
Commodore Perry Hotel 103, 139
Community Traction Company 41
Confederate prisoners 32
Consaul Street 58, 127, 131
Corey Road Field 148
Cornell, Don
Coyle Funeral Home 35
Cribb Lights 27
Crimson Coaches 35
Crosby, Bing 11
Croxton House for Nurses 101
Culinary Institute of America 12
Curtice 14

D
Dana Corporation 130
Darin, Bobby 111
"Daring Young Man on the Flying Trapeze" 65
Defender, The 32
Defiance 54
Delaware Avenue 121
Delence Street 76
Delux carryout 69, 122
DeLuxe Cleaners 81
Dempsey, William "Jack" 28; Dempsey-Willard fight 28
Detroit Avenue 4, 14, 45, 87, 116, 148
Detroit Harvester Company 148
Detroit Tigers 109
Diaper Service 111
Dietrich, Marlene 97
District Nurse Association 42
Doehler-Jarvis Co. 114
Dogs 30, 113
Don's Drive-in 121
Don & Mel's Drive-In 121
Dorr Street 48, 101, 102, 115
Douglas Road 36, 111, 134
Drive-in restaurants 121, 142
Drum and bugle corps 43
Drugstores 1, 17, 90, 101, 103
Duck Creek 18
Dunbar Center 72
Dura Corporation 148

E
East Broadway 86
Eastern Airlines 151
East Side 16, 96
East Side Auto Parts 60
East Side Hospital 113
East Toledo 1, 2, 8, 14, 44, 55, 60, 74, 86
Eight o'clock coffee 71
Electric Auto-Lite 103, 130
Elephants 94
El Greco 141
Ellington, Duke 96
Ellis Ambulance Service 127
El Pinto restaurant 75
Emerald Street 365
Eppes Essen Restaurant 121
Erie Street 16, 17, 48, 127; Erie (South) 91
Essex, U.S.S. 21
Euclid Avenue 8, 61
Excelsior Auto-Cycles 29

F
Factories 19, 25, 72, 103, 107, 130, 148
Falstaff beer 119
Farr, Jamie 145
Fassett Street Bridge 142
Fearing Boulevard 25, 64
Feilbach, Charles 42
Feilbach School 42
Ferries, Greyhound inside front cover; Pastime 8
Finlay Brewing 26
Fire vehicles 17, 33
Fire stations 17, 19, 33, 35
First St. John Lutheran Church
First Street 60
First Unitarian Church 43
Fiske Brothers Refinery 96
Fitzgerald, Ella 111
Floods 18, 23
Football 11, 39, 62, 87, 100, 151
Ford Model A 59; Model T 49
Forest Cemetery 26
Foth-Dorfmeyer Funeral Home 33
Foth Funeral Home 33
Franciscan Sisters 54

Franklin Elementary School 1
Freighters 13, 27, 142
Front Street 8, 40, 55, 74, 104, 127, 131
Funeral homes 33, 35
Fun Farm 126

G
GAR (see Grand Army of the Republic)
GI Bill 115
Garbe Block 1
Gas stations 62, 90, 105, 127
Gaynor, Mitzi 122
Gaylords, The 120
Genesee Street 16, 58
Georgia Avenue 90
Gibbons Street 17
Gibson Band 91
Girard Street 72
Girl Scouts 43, 54
Gladieux coal yard 71
Glassmaking 22, 114
Glendale Avenue 4, 14, 30
Glendale-Feilbach School 42
Glenn, Jean 18
Golf 14, 50, 67
Goon's Drugs 101
Goon Ice Cream 101
Grand Army of the Republic 1, 15, 24,
Grand Rapids 23
Gray's Home Made Mayonnaise & Sandwich Spread 37
Great American Tea Company 71
Great Atlantic and Pacific Tea Company 71
Greyhound, the – inside front cover
Grocers 12, 16, 36, 38, 42, 43, 48, 52, 69, 71, 82, 87, 91, 102, 112

H
Harlem Globetrotters 120
Harvard Elementary School 4
Hasty Hill Farm 149
Hawley Hardware 119
Hawley Street 119
Highland Park 45
High Level Bridge 56
Hirsch bookstore 89, News

153

Agency 36, newsstand 36, 89
Hirzel Greenhouse 135
Hoag Street 62
Hobart Street 91
Holden, William 122
Holy Trinity Greek Orthodox Cathedral 133
Hopewell School 137
Horses 12, 17, 18, 26, 28, 35, 56, 83, 136
Hospitals 14, 37, 40, 45, 113
Hotels 26, 83, 103, 139
Hudson Terraplane 105
Huron Street 106, 118

I
Ice boating, 99
Ice delivery 78
International Park 8
Interurban Line 30, 53
Inverness Country Club 50
Ironville 14
Iwo Jima 25

J
Jack Frost Sugars 62
Jackman Road 137
Jackson Street 112
Jane Parker Foods 71
Jeep 72, 95, 97, 105, 107, 127
Jeep Parkway 125
Jefferson Avenue 15, 17, 34, 40, 61, 91
Jerome Street 63
Johnny Dark 134
Jokinen, Eli 71
Johnson's Island 32
Judges 6, 67, 77, 87, 97, 111

K
Kaiser 127; Kaiser Frazer 134
Kennedy, Jack 114
Ketcham horse farm 28
King Guillame I 22
Kin-Wa-Low 98, 110, 111
Kirby, Durward 119
Kmart 70, 94
Knudel's grocery store 102
Koerber Brewery 74
Kopf, Edgar A. repair shop 21
Krantz Brewing Company 114

Kresge, S.S. 36, 70
Kroger Grocery & Baking Co. 48
Kruse's Saloon 22
Kuehmann Potato Chip Co. 69, 106, 115
Kurtz Meat Market 12

L
Lagrange Street 114, 117
Labor Day 135
Lady of the Lake 116
Lagrange Street 145
Lake Erie 27, 52
Lakefront Dock & Railroad Terminal 118
Lamson's 91, 117
Lasalle's 117, 147
Lawrence Avenue 43, 48, 90
Leroy's Market 127
Leroy's Towing 127
Lewis Avenue 55, 105
Libbey Cowboys 100
Libbey, Edward Drummond 22, 54, 64, 100; Florence Scott 54, 64, 100
Libbey Glass factory 22
Libbey High School 100
Libbey-Owens-Ford 114
Liberty Theatre 4
Licavoli Gang 114
Lincoln Cleaners 81
Lindbergh, Charles 51
Lighthouses 27
Lincoln Avenue 48
Linker Tire & Supply Co. 55
Lion Dry Goods Co. 52
Lion Store 52, 117
Liveries 12
Locust Street 37
Logan's Carryout 134
Lor, Denise 149
Losser Pharmacy 90
Lourdes College 54
Lucas County 118
Lucas County Courthouse –cover photo, preface
Lucas County Armory 5, 11
Lucas County Recreation Center 150
Lumpers 68
Lutheran Home Society 2
Lutheran Orphans Home 2

M
M&R Lunch 80
Mackinaw 40, 104
Macomber Vocational School 110, 115
Madison Avenue 70, 84, 99, 109, 147
Magnolia Street 103
Main Library 113
Main Street (Toledo) 1, 8, 55, 60, 66; (Bowling Green) 23
Major League Baseball 109
Manhattan Boulevard 94, 117
Maplewood Avenue 42
Marionettes 92
Maumee (city of) 37
Maumee Bay 26, cabins 133; sailing 56, 99
Maumee Bay Range Lights 27
Maumee Cemetery 18
Maumee River 54; boats 8, 52, 83, 140; floods 18; homes 4; navigation 27
Maumee Valley Hospital 45
Mayors 63, 67, 91, 97, 136
May Coal Company 62
McCreary's Point 32
Melody C Choir 93
Mel's Drive-In 142
Memorial Day 91, 129
Mercy Hospital 40, 113
Metroparks 97
Metzger's Dry Goods 1, 98
Meyer Drug Co. 103
Miami-Erie Canal 97
Miami Street 135
Michigan Street 22, 39, 58, 87, 103
Middle Bass Island 52
Midget racers 150
Monoky Café 16
Monroe Street 10, 43, 48, 87, 90, 111, 120, 123, 127
Monroe, Vaughan and his Orchestra 149
Moore, Garry TV Show 119, 149
Motorcycles 29, 92
Mt. Carmel Cemetery 117
Mt. Nebo Church 4
Mud Hens 44, 109, 120
Music 25, 34, 43, 91, 93, 96, 114

N
Nabisco elevators 58
Nash Rambler 132
National Association of Letter Carriers 34
National School of Meat Cutting 12
Native American 14
Naval Training School 83
Naval training ship 21
Navarre Avenue 105
Nebraska Avenue 33, 48, 82
Nehrig, Howard J. 69, 106, 107, 115
Nevada Street 86
New Hope Methodist Church 35, 129, 140
Newspapers 42, 61, 66, 75, 144
New York Yankees 109
Nissen coal yard 71
North 12th Street 141
North Cove Boulevard 101
Norwood Avenue 69, 122, 127
Notre Dame 22, Academy 138
Nurses 101, 107,

O
Oak Grove Place 77, 95
Oak Street 60, 74, 113
Oakdale Avenue 96
Oakwood Avenue 48
Oatis Avenue 101
O'Connell, Helen 111
Ohio Adjutant General's Department 21
Ohio Building 94
Ohio Centennial Exposition 26
Ohio Naval Militia 24
Ohio State 22
Okun Produce 68
Old Dutch Beer 114
Old Newsboys 61; band 10; scholarships, 111
Old Timers 50
Old West End 124
Oliver House 5
Oliver Street 5
"One-Eyed, One-Horned Flying Purple People Eater" 144
Ontario Street 78, 102, 111, 129
Orchard Street 2

Oregon Road 135
Osterman & Levey Jewelers 84, 85
Ottawa County 14
Ottawa Park golf course 67;
Ottawa River 32
Overland Model 38, 25
Owens-Illinois 78, 146

P
Packo's Central Kitchen 127; restaurant 58
Page Diary 44
Page Field 44
Page Street 63
Paine Avenue 79
Parades 10, 24, 26, 91, 99, 108, 110, 114, 116, 117, 122, 129, 133, 135, 145
Parks 28, 45, 46, 50, 97
Parkside Boulevard 102
Parkwood Avenue 28
Pastime 8
Paul Whiteman Orchestra 11
Pedestrian mall 147
Pee Wee League 119
Pharmacies (see Drugstores)
Philadelphia Orchestra 64
Phillips Avenue 105
Phillips grocery store 71
Picnics 21, 46, 52, 97, 107
Pie Eater's Club 125
Pier Marquette railroad yard 71
Pilots 51
Pinewood Avenue 57, 89, 93
Pittsburgh Paints 119
Plumey Block 1, 8
Poinsettia Street 143
Point Place 37, 53
Police (see Toledo Police)
Polio 42
Polo club 148
Pope Auto 27
Pope-Toledo 25
Port Authority 111
Postal Service band 34; carriers 6, 34, 89; contract pilots 51; stations 6, 10, 34, 66, 108
Presidents Eisenhower 133; Lincoln 87; McKinley preface; Roosevelt 138; Taft 6
Presley, Elvis 139

Presque Isle 8
"Pride of Toledo" 8
Produce 38, 68, 86, 106, 107, 124
Prohibition 26, 74
Prouty Street 27
Public transportation 18, 25, 30, 41, 53
Pure Oil Company 62
Put-in-Bay 19
Putt-Putt 111

Q

R
Radbone Hotel 26; Ned 26
Rahe Grocery 76
Railroads 18, 25, 30, 71, 118; miniature 136
Rambler 132
Rambo Lane 28
Raymer Street 41
Restaurants 68, 75, 80, 98, 111, 127, 131, 133, 141
Rhythm Boys 11
Ringling Bros. Barnum & Bailey Circus 94
River Road 4
Riverside Park 107
Rivoli Theater 134
Roberts, Emma 42
Robinwood Avenue 37
Robinwood Hospital 37
Roller coasters 15, 32, 33
Rotary Club 42
Roth Pontiac 126
Roundhouse 25
Royal Venetians 96
Rucki's Market 91

S
Safety Building 50, 59, 63
St. Claire Academy, Hall 54
St. Clair Street 48, 70, 80, 89, 94, 108
St. Emery Society 119
St. John College 22
St. John Lutheran Church 2
St. John University 22
St. John's Evangelical Lutheran Church 49
St. John's High School 22
St. Louis Browns 109

154

St. Luke's Hospital 37
St. Mary's 63
St. Stanislas School 25
St. Stephen's 58, 119
Scenic, The 15
Schiff Shoes 66
Schmidt Meats 116
Schneck Coal Company 5
Schools 4, 11, 18, 22, 25, 39, 42, 50, 62, 63, 89, 100, 137, 144, 152
Scott High School, Jesup W. 11, 39, 146, 152
Scott Park 50; race track 150
Sealtest Dairy 136
Seaman Road 2, 49
Secor Road 149
Secrets 36
Shaw, Artie 96
Sherbrooke Restaurant 141
Sheriff's deputy 119
Sherman Street 101
Ships 8, 13, 19, 21, 27, 40, 56, 74, 104, 118
Shipyards 74, 104
Side Cut Park 97
Silvercup Bakery 102
Silver Moon Café 76
Sinclair gas station 127
Sixth Street 8
Smead Avenue 127
Softball 62
Sohio 62
Somerset United Brethren Church 3; E.U.B 140
South Avenue 103
South Avenue Bridge 45
South Toledo 30, 91, 124
Spanish-American War 5, preface
Spieker Company, Henry J. 18
Spielbusch Avenue 5, 11
Spicer Manufacturing Company 130, 134
Spitzer Building 99
Sports 11, 16, 22, 39, 44, 50, 56, 62, 71, 87, 109, 120
Sports Arena 132, 139
Springbrook Polo Club 148
Stadium Road 49
Standard Oil of Ohio 62
Starr Avenue 29, 41

State Guard 91
State Hospital 14
Steinman Auto Repair 129
Stengel, Casey 44
Stokowski, Leopold 64
Streetcars 41, 53; tracks 21, 23
Suder Avenue 16
Sugar Island 52
Suko Hall 7
Sullivan, Ed 128
Summit Street 5, 6, 7, 26, 36, 38, 55, 6, 70, 84
Sunday, Billy 11
Sunshine Children's Home 111
Superior Street 10, 22, 24, 29, 48, 55, 84, 109, 133, 138
Swan, The 86
Swan Creek 45, 100
Swayne Field 44, 87, 120
Swayne, Noah 87
Sylvania Avenue 33, 81, 120, 120, 148
Sylvania (village of) 54

T
Taft, William Howard 6
TARTA (see Toledo Area Regional Transit Authority)
Taste of the Town 128
Taynor, Agnes, family 16
Ted's Hamburger 127
Teen Town 137
Ten Mile Creek 32
Theaters 4, 15, 75, 80, 134
Third Baptist Church 89, 93
Thanksgiving Day 143, 146
Tiedtke's 82, 84, 92, 109, 113, 117, 149, inside back cover
Tiny Tot Diaper Service 111
Toledo Area Boy Scout Council 106
Toledo Area Regional Transit Authority 41
Toledo (Transcontinental Airport of) 51
Toledo Beach 17
Toledo Bowling Hall of Fame 16
Toledo Council of Social Agencies 128
Toledo Division of Parks, Boulevards and Recreation 50
Toledo Express 126, 151

Toledo Fire Department 17, 19
Toledo Hospital, The School of Nursing 101
Toledo Letter Carriers Band 34
Toledo Maroons 11
Toledo Mercury team 120
Toledo Municipal Airport 92
Toledo Museum of Art 43, 54, 64
Toledo News 61
Toledo News-Bee 61
Toledo Newsboys 138; band 19
Toledo Police Department 24; Bureau of Identification 24, 59
Toledo Scale 123, 135
Toledo Shipbuilding Company 40, 74
Toledo skyline 140
Toledo Spain Plaza 15, 110
Toledo Sports, Home, Food and Auto Show 128
Toledo Telegraph and Telephone Messenger Co. 58
Toledo Testing Labs 141
Toledo Times 42, 67
Toledo Training School 101
Toledo Trust 109; Building 36, 84, 108
Toledo Zoning Board 111
Toledo Zoo, The 15, 22, 30, 136, 138, 145; aviary 146; talking storybooks 146; Wonder Valley 139, 145, 150
Transcontinental Airport of Toledo 51
Tremainsville Road 36
Triangle Hamburger 87
Trianon Ballroom 96
Trolleys (see Streetcars)
Turtle Island 27

U
U Haul 127
UAW-CIO 135
Unions 22, 34, 135
Union Station 122
United Way 111
United Nations 77
University Hall 50
University of Toledo, The 50, 87, 137
Upton Avenue 69, 90, 122
United Veterans Memorial Association 117
Universal Commercial Investment Trust 132
University Circle 137
Utah Street 56

V
Valentine Theater 80
Val St. Lambert Glass Works 22
Van's Market 87
Vance Street 71
Vermont Street 113
VFW 117
Victory Day 99, 110
Virginia Street
Vistula 133
Vollmar Park 46, 83
Volunteers of America 111

W
Wabash & Erie Canal 26
Wager Brothers 90
Waite High School, Morrison R 11, 18, 39, 62, 131, 146
Walbridge Park 15, 42, 70, 86, 105, 138
Walnut Street 6, 133
Walton Brothers Bakery 48
Wamba Festival 10
War Bonds 97, 109
Washington Senators 109
Washington Street 132
Washington Township 149
Anthony Wayne (High Level) Bridge 56; Trail 30
Wayne Street 35, 64, 140
Webster's market 42
Weiler Homes 4
Wernert, J.E. grocery 36
Wernerts Corners 36
Western Avenue 129
Western Avenue Methodist Church 35, 129, 140
Westgate Shopping Center 149
Westminster Church 22
Wheaties 109
Wheeling Street 2
Whip, The 86, 105
White Company 40
White, Jim 116
Whiteman Orchestra, Paul 11
White Trucks Sales & Service 40

Whitney Vocational School, Harriet 110
Whittemore Street 16
Wildwood Addition 30
Willard, Jess 28
Willys 74, 127
Willis Day Storage Company 130
Willys-Overland 19, 25, 60, 72, 73, 95, 105, 107, 123, 125, 127, 128, 143, 150
Willys Parkway 49, 65
Women's Overseas Service League 95
Women's Hospital 14
Woodill Wildfire 134
Woodlawn Cemetery 61
Woodley 33
East Woodruff Avenue 113
Woodville Road 56, 105
Woodward, Calvin M. 39
Woodward High School, Calvin M. 39, 42, 144
Woodward Technical School 39, 42
World Series 1945 109
World's Fair 78
Woolworth, F.W. 147
Wright Brothers Wholesale 137
WPA 30, 70, 145, 146
WSPD 126, 132

X

Y
YMCA 77
Yost Street 19
Yuma 13

Z
Zip'z Ice Cream 111
Zoo, The Toledo (see listing under Toledo)
Zimmerman Blacksmith 12

SUBMITTER INDEX

A
Adkins, D. 43
Amidon, Jeanny 51, 53, 114
Aranyosi, Andrew 79

Arnold, Carol (Hillebrand) 22, 32, 86, 148
Ashton, Paula 120

B
Bachar, Barbara (Varkoly) 136
Bartus, Amy 68
Baumgartner, Douglas 121
Beaudry, Dale 108
Beavers-Deck, Kathy 6
Beham, Mary K. (Mrs. Walter) 81
Belding, Jeanne 41
Bigland, Jim 107, 143
Binkowski, Mary Ann and Stephen 102, 110, 118, 122, 145, 146, 150
Blum, James 14
Boehk, Louis 18, 21
Born, Ron 44
Brown, Donald 113
Brown, Joyce (Gibson) 91, 93
Bryan, Rick 51, 53, 56, 114
Buchholtz, Evelyn (Oswald) 77, 143

C
Callejas, Melissa 69
Calmes, Connie 29, 97
Campbell, Stuart 95
Campbell-Potts, Grace 65, 77, 95
Carr, Carolyn (Langel) 127
Chambers, Berniece 57
Clark, Joanne 40, 74
Collier, Winona 150
Connors, John 10, 134

D
Damaskas, the Rev. Aristotle 133
Davis, Naomi 82, 100, 116
Defon, Refa 114
Drake, Sandra 40, 117
Drayton, LaRoyna (Hardnett) 127
Drozdowicz, Madeline (Larberg) 105

E
Eberly, Dolores (Baker) 29, 55, 88, 125
Evanoff, Alice (Palmiter) 131, 134
Ewing, Anne (Logan) 134

F
Fiddler, Robert 16
Fischer, Mary 80

G
Gable, Ronald 24, 27
Gauthier, Corrine 4, 85, 101, 123, 132, 138
Gibbs, Kenneth P. 28
Girl Scout Council of Maumee Valley 43, 54, 93
Goldberg, Al 120
Goldie, Frank 152
Good, Mary 2, 4, 33, 35
Gracheck, Ted 114
Graumlich, Al 49

H
Hankison, John E. "Jack" 148
Hanley, Joseph P. II 106, 128
Harrison, Phillip R. 17
Heilbrun, Louis and Vera 113, 149
Hendrickson, Charlotte Carr 96
Heydinger, Norman 61
Hillabrand, Tom 105
Hirsch, Gordon 36, 89
Hirzel, Robert 135
Holden, Olivia 142
Holland, Louise 149
Holman, Judith 40, 117
Holman, Judy and Mel 99
Holy Trinity Greek Orthodox Cathedral 133
Hoot, Etta (Edelman) 7, 23, 52
Horner, Lois (Holtz) 26, 32
Horner, Sarah 26, 32
Huber, Terry 96
Hurley, Jeannette (Barba) 119
Husman, Sandy 130

I
Ignasiak, Shirley 109

J
Jackson, Ken 46
Jarzynski, Christine 115, 117, 145
Jarzynski, Leo 115
Johnson, Kathleen (You) 133
Johnston, Mike 136

K
Kanapek, Ted 129
Kaufman, Helen 124
Kirk, Peggy 147
Klausing, Kathy (Bowser) 147
Kluender, Candace 127
Kramer, Robin (Oberdorf) 66
Kubiak, Kevin 137
Kunz, Rick 27
Kutz, Fred 98, 133

L
Labuhn, the Rev. Gerald H. 2
Lajeunesse, Joseph 50
Langenderfer, Bernice (Baker) 83
Lasko, Frank "Whitey" 119
Lefevre, Robert Gaston 22
Lengel, Terrence 62
Levinson, Lily, Manny, Sid 121
Levey, Bob 84, 85
Liebeherr, Mary 1, 8
Ligibel, Nancy 22, 86
Lindsey, Irene 148
Long, Tedd 61
Loo, Howard 98, 99
Loo, John 110
Loo, Myrna and Howard 111
Lourdes College 54
Lynch, Doris (Stewart) 130

M
T.V. Mangan 118
Manion, Mike 125, 138
Manore, Evelyn 139
Maxfield, Shirley 78, 112
Maxwell, Micaela 144
McCarthy, Beverly 30
McCracken, Lloyd 42
Meyer, Robert 103
Michael, Dorothy 25
Mills, Ken 16, 20; Lavern "Vern" 20
Miner, Beverly 43, 54, 93
Mioduszczewski, Dorothy 129
Moritz, Roy 49, 71
Moulton, Irving "Bud" 76
Mucci, Harold 8, 15, 21, 142
Myers, El 19

N
Nagy, Julius 104
Nehrig, Ruth 69, 80, 106, 107, 115
New Hope United Methodist Church 35, 129, 140
Nickoloff, Judy (Jokinen) 17, 77,144
Niese, Connie 34

O
Okun, Fred 10, 11, 12, 68
O'Shea, Anne 97

P
Pack, Joyce 70, 137
Packo Tony 131
Pfaff, Judy 116, 123, 124, 125, 126
Prisby, Ted 112, 116
Purnia, Delphine 86, 105

Q

R
Ravin, Sharon 66
Rankin, David 78
Rehfeldt, Paul 91
Ricci, Sue 13, 15
Richards, Bob 138
Riley, James and Rosemary (McGarry) 42
Roach, Equilla (Gibson) 89, 91
Rockwell, Cynthia (Erskine) 64
Rumpf, Joan 50, 92, 107
Rutter, Tom 33, 39, 139

S
Saba, Sally 12, 38, 87
Sackman, Barbara 74, 103
St. Luke's Hospital 37
Sample, Pamela D. 64, 141
Schaefer, Robert 5, 55, 94
Schott, Nancy (Bella) Brown 109
Schmuhl, Jerry 118
Schramm, Helen 80
Schwab, Delbert 21
Sepanski, Linda Schroeder 140
Shnider, Ron 111
Sheets, Helene 54, 91
Shook, Judy (Lebowsky) 36, 37, 58, 63
Sitzmann, H. Martin and Ruth 75
Slowinski, Dolores "Dee" (Lendecker) 25, 101, 135
Smeltzer, Ruth 82, 90
Smith, Don and Ginny 92
Stover, Nancy 24, 59, 63
Sugg, Ann-Marie, Elizabeth, and Gary 45
Szymanski, Chester R. 62, 70, 72, 113, 119

T
Taylor, Denny 56, 102
Taylor, Jim 78
Taylor, Marilee 35, 129, 140
Toledo Yacht Club 27
Torrence, Glen 18, 26

U
Uhrman, Robert 50

V
VanGunten, Roger 30, 120
Venzke, David 28
Voller, Cindy M. 60, 67

W
Wagar, Mrs. Jack 90
Walsh, Rebecca 121
Walton, David 48
Warner, Connie 8, 15, 21, 142
Wasserman, Mary Ann 45
Welborn, Jane (Bryan), Sara 152
Western Lake Erie Historical Society 27
Westphal, Ron 94, 126
Wherry, Jennifer 7, 73
Whitaker, Lorean Quinn 72
Williamson, Carmen 76
Wing, Linda 112, 126
Wirebaugh, Jeffrey 19
Wodarski, Tom 151
Wyatt, Bill 128, 132
Wyatt, Janet (Quinn) 146

X

Y
Yaros, Sharon 14, 23
You, Wayne 133

Z
Ziegler, Perry 87
Zouhary, Tom 141

BIBLIOGRAPHY

Bend of The River Magazine

Buchholz, Richard H. *The History of The Old Newsboys Goodfellow Association*, 2000.

Hage, Robyn and Michaels, Larry R. *A Chance for Every Child; History of Toledo Public Schools*, 2003.

Ligibel, Ted, *The Toledo Zoo's First 100 Years, A Century of Adventure*, 1999.

Manufacturing and Mercantile Resources of Toledo, South Toledo, and Perrysburg, 1882.

Michaels, Larry R. *East Side Story: People & Places in the History of East Toledo*, 1993.

Mosier-Porter, Tana. *Toledo Profile: A Sesquicentennial History*, 1987.

The Ohio Historical Society

The Toledo Bee

The Toledo Blade

Toledo City Directories

Toledo History Scrapbooks, The Toledo-Lucas County Public Library.

Toledo Monitor

The Toledo News-Bee

Toledo Police Division, 1867-1977, Volume II.

Toledo Police Division, 1867-1992, Volume III.

The Toledo Sunday Journal

The Toledo Times

United States Federal Census